The
Translator

The
Translator

A Tribesman's Memoir
of Darfur

Daoud Hari

*As told to Dennis Michael Burke
and Megan M. McKenna*

RANDOM HOUSE   NEW YORK

2008 Random House International Edition

Published in the United States by Random House,
an imprint of The Random House Publishing Group,
a division of Random House, Inc., New York.

RANDOM HOUSE and colophon are registered
trademarks of Random House, Inc.

Originally published in hardcover in the United States
by Random House, Inc., New York, in 2008.

LIBRARY OF CONGRESS CATALOGING-IN-PUBLICATION DATA

Hari, Daoud.
The translator: a tribesman's memoir of Darfur / Daoud Hari.
p.   cm.
ISBN 978-0-8129-7959-6
1. Hari, Daoud.   2. Translators—Sudan—Darfur—Biography.
3. Sudan—History—Darfur Conflict, 2003—Personal narratives,
Sudanese.   I. Title.
DT159.6.D27H38 2008
962.404'3092—dc22
[B]   2007042308

Printed and bound in the United States of America
on acid-free paper

www.atrandom.com

1 2 3 4 5 6 7 8 9

Book design by Carole Lowenstein

*To my mother and all
the women of Darfur*

Contents

Introduction

"If God must break your leg He will at least teach you to limp"—so it is said in Africa. This book is my poor limping, a modest account that cannot tell every story that deserves telling. I have seen and heard many things in Darfur that have broken my heart. I bring the stories to you because I know most people want others to have good lives, and, when they understand the situation, they will do what they can to steer the world back toward kindness. This is when human beings, I believe, are most admirable.

If you know where Egypt is on the map, you can go down from there and find Sudan. The western side of Sudan is called Darfur, which is about the size of France or Texas. Darfur is mostly flat; it has a few mountains but many endless plains of little trees, scratchy bushes, and sandy streambeds.

Darfur is where I lived with my family until the attack on our village. Our people are called the Zaghawa. We are traditional tribal herdsmen who live in permanent villages; our grass huts are very big around and have pointed roofs that smell very good in the rain. My childhood was as full of happy adventures as yours. While you probably had a bicycle and then a first car, I had a camel, Kelgi, that I loved dearly and could make go very fast. On cold nights he might come into the hut, which was okay with everyone.

While we Zaghawa are not Arabs, many nomadic Arabs lived near us and were a part of my childhood as friends. My father took me to feasts in their tents, and they feasted with us.

Dar means land. The *Fur* are tribespeople farther south who are mostly farmers. One of the Fur leaders was king of the whole region in the 1500s. The region took its name from that time.

Hundreds of thousands of my people have been killed recently, as you may know. Two and a half million others are now living difficult lives in refugee camps or in solitary hiding places in desert valleys. I will explain why this is happening. If you are hungry for more details, I have included a deeper explanation in the back of this book.

As for the future, the only way that the world can say no to genocide is to make sure that the people of Darfur are returned to their homes and given protection. If the world allows the people of Darfur to be removed forever from their land and their way of life, then genocide will happen elsewhere because it will be seen as something that works. It must not be allowed to work. The people of Darfur need to go home now.

I write this for them, and for that day, and for a particular woman and her three children in heaven, and for a particular man and his daughter in heaven, and for my own father and my brothers in heaven, and for those still living who might yet have beautiful lives on the earth.

I write this also for the women and girls of Darfur. You have seen their faces wrapped in beautiful colors, and you know something of their suffering, but they are not who you think. Though they have been victimized, they are heroes more than victims. My aunt Joyar, for example, was a famous warrior who dressed like a man, fought camel thieves and Arab armies, wrestled men for sport—and always won. She refused to marry until she was in her forties. I dedicate this to her and to the girls of my village who were faster and stronger than the boys at our rough childhood games. I dedicate this to my mother, who, as a young woman, kept a circle of attacking lions away from our cattle and sheep in the bush for a long day, a long night, and all the next morning, using only the power of her voice and the banging of two sticks. The power of her voice is something I know very well.

Near my village is a beautiful mountain we have always called the Village of God. Though the Muslim religion is practiced throughout our area both by indigenous Africans like me and by Arab nomads, it is also true that our people, especially our young people, have always gone up on this mountain to put offerings into the small holes of the rocks. Meat, millet, or wildflowers may be placed in these holes, along with letters to God, thanking Him or asking Him please for some favor. These gifts and notes have been left here long before the newer religions came to us. For a young man or woman, a letter may ask that some other young person be chosen for his or her mate. It might be a letter asking that a grandfather's illness be cured, or that the rainy season be a good one, or that a wedding be beautiful and the marriage successful. Or it might simply ask that the year ahead be good for everyone in the village below. So here it is, God: I am up there now in my heart, and I put this book in Your mountain as an offering to You. And I praise You by all Your Names, and I praise our ancient Mother of the Earth, and all the Prophets and wise men and women and Spirits of heaven and earth who might help us now in our time of need.

And for you, my friend, my reader, I thank you so much for taking this journey. It is a hard story, of course, but there are many parts that I think will surprise you and make you very happy that you came with me.

The story I am telling here is based on my memories of a time of great difficulty and confusion. I have done my best to capture the details of my experiences, and to set them down here accurately and to the utmost of my recollection, and I am grateful to those who have helped me focus and occasionally correct my account. Of course, no two people can view the same event in the same way, and I know that others will have their own tales to tell. Surely these collective tales will add up to the truth of the tragedy in Darfur.

The
Translator

1.
A Call from
the Road

I am sure you know how important it can be to get a good phone signal. We were speeding through the hot African desert in a scratched and muddy Land Cruiser that had been much whiter a week earlier. Our driver, a Darfur tribesman like me, was swerving through thorny acacia bushes, working the gears expertly in the deep sands of another and always another ravine, which we call a wadi, and sailing over the bumps in the land—there are no roads to speak of. In the backseat, a young news filmmaker from Britain, Philip Cox, was holding on as we bounced and as our supplies thumped and clanked and sloshed around. A veteran of these deserts, he was in good humor—even after a long week of dusty travel and so many emotionally difficult interviews. Survivors told us of villages surrounded at night by men with torches and machine guns, the killing of men, women, and children, the burning of people alive in the grass huts of Darfur. They told us of the rape and mutilation of young girls, of execution by ma-chete of young men—sometimes eighty at a time in long lines.

You cannot be a human being and remain unmoved, yet if it is your job to get these stories out to the world, you keep going. So we did that.

I was Philip's translator and guide, and it was my job to keep us alive. Several times each hour I was calling military commanders from rebel groups or from the Chad National Army to ask if we should go this way or that way to avoid battles or other trouble. My great collection of phone num-bers was the reason many reporters trusted me to take them into Darfur. I don't know how Philip got my cell number in the first place—maybe from the U.S. Embassy, or the U.S. State Department, or the British Embassy, or from the U.N. High Commissioner for Refugees, or from one of the aid organizations or a resistance group. It seemed that every-one had my cell phone number now. He certainly did not get my number from the government of Sudan, whose sol-diers would kill me if they caught me bringing in a reporter.

These satellite phone calls—and often just cell phone calls—frequently were to commanders who said, *No, you will die if you come here, because we are fighting so-and-so today.* We would then find another way.

If one rebel group hears that you have been calling an-other group, they might think you are a spy, even though you are only doing this for the journalist and for the story—you give the rebels nothing in return. I had to be careful about such things if I wanted to get my reporters out of Darfur alive, and so more stories could go out to the world. Since the attack on my own village, that had become my reason, and really my only reason, for living. I was feeling mostly dead inside and wanted only to make my remaining days count for something. You have perhaps felt this way at some time. Most of the young men I had grown up with were now dead or fighting in the resistance; I, too, had chosen to risk myself, but was using my English instead of a gun.

We needed to arrive at our destination before sundown or risk attack by the Sudanese Army, or by Darfur rebels aligned with government, or by other rebels who didn't know who we were and who might kill us just to be safe. So we didn't like what happened next.

Our Land Cruiser was suddenly blocked by six trucks that emerged from a maze of desert bushes. These were Land Cruisers, too, but with their roofs cut off completely so men could pile in and out instantly, as when they have to escape a losing battle or get out before a rocket-propelled grenade (RPG) reaches them. Dusty men with Kalashnikov rifles piled out. On the order of their commander, they pointed their guns at us. When so many guns are pulled ready at the same time, the crunching sound is memorable. We moved slowly out of our vehicle with our hands raised.

These men were clearly rebel troops: their uniforms were but dirty jeans; ammunition belts hung across their chests; their loosely wrapped turbans, or *shals*—head scarves, really—were caked with the dust of many days' fighting. No doctors travel with these troops, who fight almost every day and leave their friends in shallow graves.

Emotionally, they are walking dead men who count their future in hours. This makes them often ruthless, as if they think everyone might as well go to the next life with them. Many of them have seen their families murdered and their villages burned. You can imagine how you would feel if your hometown were wiped away and all your family killed by an enemy whom you now roam the land to find and kill so you can die in peace.

Among the rebels are the Sudan Liberation Movement, the Sudan Liberation Army, the Justice and Equality Movement, and several others. There are other groups in Chad, and they travel across the borders as they please. Where they get their guns and money is often a mystery, but Darfur has been filled with automatic weapons from the time when Libya attacked Chad and used Darfur as a staging area. Also, it must be understood that Sudan is aligned with radical Islamic groups and is, as a separate matter, letting China get most of its oil. So some Western interests and some surrounding countries are thought to be involved in supporting the rebel groups. It is sad how ordinary people suffer when these chess games are played.

Nearly half of Africa is covered by the pastoral lands of herding villages, and much of this land has great wealth below and poor people above. They are among the three hundred million Africans who earn less than a dollar a day, and who are often pushed out of the way or killed for such things as oil, water, metal ore, and diamonds. This makes the rise of rebel groups very easy. The men who stopped us probably needed no persuasion to join this group.

The men's weary-looking young commander walked to me and said in the Zaghawa language, "Daoud Ibarahaem Hari, we know all about you. You are a spy. I know you are Zaghawa like us, not Arab, but unfortunately we have some orders, and we have to kill you now."

It was easy for him to know I was a Zaghawa from the small scars that look like quotation marks and were cut into my temples by my grandmother when I was an infant. I told him yes, I am Zaghawa, but I am no spy.

The commander breathed in a sad way and then put the muzzle of his M-14 rifle to one of these scars on my head. He asked me to hold still and told Philip to stand away. He paused to tell Philip in broken English not to worry, that they would send him back to Chad after they killed me.

"Yes, fine, but just a sec," Philip replied, holding his hand up to stop the necessary business for a moment while he consulted me.

"What is going on?"

"They think I am a spy, and they are going to shoot the gun and it will make my head explode, so you should stand away."

"Who are they?" he asked.

I told him the name of the group, nodding carefully in the direction of a vehicle that had their initials hand-painted on the side.

He looked at the vehicle and lowered his hands to his hips. He looked the way the British look when they are upset by some unnecessary inconvenience. Philip wore a well-wrapped turban; his skin was tanned and a little cracked from his many adventures in these deserts. He was not going to stand by and lose a perfectly good translator.

"Wait just a moment!" he said to the rebel commander. "*Do . . . not . . . shoot . . . this . . . man.* This man is not a spy. This man is my translator and his name is Suleyman Abakar Moussa of Chad. He has his papers." Philip thought that was my name. I had been using that name to avoid being deported from Chad to a certain death in Sudan, where I was wanted, and to avoid being otherwise forced to stay in a Chad refugee camp, where I could be of little service.

"I hired this man to come here; he is not a spy. We are doing a film for British television. Do you understand this? It's absolutely essential that you understand this." He asked me to translate, just to be sure, which, under my circumstance, I was happy to do.

More than his words, Philip's manner made the commander hesitate. I watched the commander's finger pet the trigger. The gun muzzle was hot against my temple. Had he fired it recently, or was it just hot from the sun? I decided that if these were about to be my last thoughts, I should try some better ones instead. So I thought about my family and how I loved them and how I might see my brothers soon.

"I am going to make a telephone call," Philip explained, slowly withdrawing his satellite phone from his khaki pants pocket. "You will not shoot this man, because your commander will talk to you on this telephone momentarily— you understand?" He looked up a number from his pocket notebook. It was the personal number of the rebel group's top commander. He had interviewed him the previous year.

"Your top man," he said to all the gunmen standing like a firing squad around us as he waited for the call to go through. "Top man. Calling his personal number now. It's ringing. Ringing and ringing."

God is good. The satellite phone had a strong signal. The number still worked. The distant commander answered his own phone. He remembered Philip warmly. Miracle after miracle.

Philip talked on the phone in a rapid English that I quietly translated for the man holding the gun.

Philip held one finger up as he spoke, begging with that finger and with his eyes for one more moment, one more moment. He laughed to show that he and the man on the phone were old friends.

"They are old friends," I translated.

Philip then held out the satellite phone to the commander, who pressed the muzzle even harder against my head.

"Please talk to him now. Please. He says it's an order for you to talk to him."

The commander hesitated as if it were some trick, but finally reached over and took the phone. The two commanders talked at length. I watched his trigger finger rise and fall like a cobra and then finally slither away. We were told to leave the country immediately.

To not get killed is a very good thing. It makes you

smile again and again, foolishly, helplessly, for several hours. Amazing. I was not shot—*humdallah*. *My brothers, you will have to wait for me a little longer.*

Our driver had been wide-eyed through all this, since drivers often do not fare well in this kind of situation. There was joy and some laughter in the Land Cruiser as we sped back toward the village of Tine—which you say "Tina"—on the Chad-Sudan border.

"That was amazing what you did," I said to Philip. We drove a few trees farther before he replied.

"Amazing, yes. Actually, I've been trying to get through to him for weeks," he said. "Lucky thing, really."

The driver, who spoke almost no English, asked me what Philip had said. I told him that he had said *God is good*, which, indeed, is what I believe he was saying.

2.
We Are
Here

Philip asked me if my name was Daoud or Suleyman. I told him that I was Daoud when in the Darfur regions of Sudan, but I was Suleyman in Chad. I explained my situation.

"Everyone has lots of names around here," was his reply. He asked what I preferred to be called. Daoud, please, though many of my close friends also call me David, which is where Daoud comes from in the Bible. I asked him for the commander's phone number, which he read to me.

We crossed back into Chad and moved up along the border, then came back into Darfur farther north. It would be worth our trouble not to run into that same rebel group again. But, one way or another, we would get the story for Philip, and Philip would get it out to the world. You have to be stronger than your fears if you want to get anything done in this life.

The problem in dealing with rebel groups is that it is often difficult to know who is on which side on any given day. The Arab government in Khartoum—the government of Sudan—makes false promises to make temporary peace with one rebel group and then another to keep the non-Arab people fighting one another. The government makes deals with ambitious commanders who are crazy enough to think the government will promote them after the war, when in fact they will be discarded if not killed then. These breakaway commanders are sometimes told to attack other rebel groups, or even to kill humanitarian workers and the troops sent from other countries to monitor compliance with cease-fire treaties. This is done so the genocide can carry on and the land can be cleared of the indigenous people. History may prove me wrong in some of these perceptions, but this is how it seems to most people who are there.

It is also believed that the government pays some of the traditional Arab people, many tribes of whom are otherwise our friends, to form deadly horseback militias called the Janjaweed to brutally kill the non-Arab Africans and burn our villages. The word *Janjaweed* may be from an ancient word meaning "faith warriors," or it may be a combination of words meaning "evil spirits on horses," or, some believe, it just means "gunmen on horseback."

This is my prediction: When the government has removed or killed all the traditional non-Arabs, then it will get the traditional Arabs to fight one another so they too will disappear from valuable lands. This is already happening in areas where the removal of non-Arab Africans is nearly complete.

"So why did you come back home to Darfur just in time for this war?" Philip asked me over the roar of the Land Cruiser as we again bounced through wadis and over sand banks.

"A very good question!" I shouted back to him with a laugh.

On a day when you come so close to death, you should think about what you are doing here. Yes, you have a job to do in this place, but maybe you are also a little crazy to be here when you could be far away. But death had been chasing me for a long time now, from when I was thirteen and the world lit up around me, and I first saw men flying in pieces above me.

Here is that story. I was finishing my afternoon chores and thinking about the coming night of playing our village games, *Anashel* and *Whee*, rough-and-tumble sports played on the moonlit sand. Twenty government troop trucks suddenly surrounded our village. The commander gathered everyone from the village and organized the beating of some of the village men—quite old men—and demanded to know the precise whereabouts of the younger men who were presumed to be hiding in the hills with the resistance groups. That in fact was where they were, but the old men did not know exactly where they were, so the commander soon realized that the beatings were useless. He burned six huts to make his point.

Changes in the weather had forced the Arab nomads to graze their animals farther south into Zaghawa lands. In the past they would have asked permission, and a few camels might have changed hands. If no bargain could be reached, and if they used the water and the grass anyway, a challenge would be made for a battle of honor on a traditional battlefield, far from any village. After that fight, the matter would be considered settled and the Arabs and the Zaghawa would immediately be friends again, dining in one another's homes.

What was different now was that the Arab government of Sudan, because it wanted the more settled people off the land, was taking sides with the Arab nomads and providing some with guns, helicopters, bombers, and tanks to decide the arguments. This had driven many of the young Zaghawa men to join resistance groups. The Sudanese Army commanders were now going from village to village, looking for these fighters, telling the women to make their men turn in their weapons or else see their homes burned. Pressure was also being put on the people to move into the towns and cities "where they would be safe." If they did this, however, they would live in the most severe kind of poverty.

The commander had grabbed me and two of my cousins to be his translators, since he knew that we were of school age and that all students were forced to learn some Arabic, which is what he spoke. If they caught you speaking Zaghawa in the schools, or not knowing your Arab words, they would use camel whips on you. The commander stood us up on the running board of his truck and made us say all his orders about giving up weapons. The women were crying and begging the soldiers to stop the beatings and let the children run away.

Often such commanders would shoot a few people to

emphasize the seriousness of the matter. In many instances, whole villages were burned. But this commander was not that strict. He told the three of us children that we must show them the way to a village he needed to visit next. We did not want to go with him, because, unlike the women and the old men who were being beaten, we knew the village defenders were in the steep wadi beyond the village waiting to attack these trucks. But we were pushed into the front seat of the first truck and were soon speeding out of the village.

Suddenly, there were painfully loud explosions all around us and machine-gun fire everywhere as the trucks came to a halt and the soldiers streamed out to find positions. We screamed from the window, "We are here! We are here! It's us!" The commander pulled us out and used us as shields as he ran into the bushes. We put our faces close to the sand and the RPG rounds exploded into some of the trucks, sending any stragglers into the sky with trails of smoke and red mists of blood. The furious gunfight seemed to go on forever, but it was actually just a few minutes: guerrilla fighters always withdraw quickly to fight another day. When the shooting stopped, the commander stood and looked down at us.

"I think you helped make a trap for me," he said, waving his pistol in our faces. We waited to die. He looked at us and, shaking his head, mumbled something we could not make out because our hearing had been hurt badly by the explosions. He then simply walked over to his men. They collected their dead and wounded and drove away in their working trucks. We ran back to the village, yelling, "We are here!" in case the defenders were still in the bushes. Our mothers and sisters greeted us, crying, dancing around us and saying so many times, *Humdallah! Thank you, God!*

The three of us couldn't hear much of anything for a few days. Eleven people died, mostly government soldiers.

Soon after that my father sent me to school in the largest city in North Darfur, El Fasher. I was his youngest son. Living with cousins, I could finish primary school and continue on to intermediate and secondary school. I was very sad to leave home.

Life in El Fasher was overwhelming—too many people, too many cars, too many new things. I got very sick the second week, mostly homesick. El Fasher is a city of mud buildings and sandy streets: so many streets that I got lost all the time. There are some government buildings and a large prison where, everyone knew, terrible things happened.

My brother Ahmed knew from our cousins that I was having a hard time, so he came to see me. He stayed for a week until I got better, walking me to school with his long arm over my shoulder and making me feel like home. He said that fate had given me a blessing, and that I should work hard at school. He came to visit whenever he could, which was quite often. He showed me good things about the town. Eventually I grew to like El Fasher.

I got a job cleaning tables at a restaurant after classes. I watched television for the first time. A cousin would put his TV outside his home so all the cousins and neighbors could watch. I didn't like it much because it was mostly about the government of Sudan's military. I did like the movies, but the first one I saw was a Clint Eastwood movie, and I went running down the street when I thought the bullets would come out of it from all the shooting. My cousins came laughing down the street to get me.

A movie house played American films once a week and films from India the rest of the time. It was very cheap; I went to see every new film with a few coins of my restaurant money.

At the restaurant, and from the older students, I began to learn about politics. There were many military operations against the Zaghawa at that time, and many Zaghawa were leaving El Fasher to join resistance groups. Dictator Omar Hassan Ahmal al-Bashir had just taken over Sudan, which made us all angry. A Chad commander named Idriss Déby was fighting the Chad government for control of that country. He is a Zaghawa and we thought he was a great hero. Some wanted to go join him. He would later become president of Chad.

This fighting sounded like a good idea to me. I dropped out of high school and hid for two weeks, planning with friends to go to Chad and join up with Déby.

Ahmed came and found me. He sat me down under a tree and told me that I should use my brain, not a gun, to make life better. He said it would be wrong to turn away from the gifts given to me by God and my family.

"Shooting people doesn't make you a man, Daoud," he said. "Doing the right thing for who you are makes you a man." So we walked back to town and I returned to school.

I became interested in English because of a wonderful teacher, and I became lost in the classic books of England and America. I particularly loved Charlotte Brontë's *Jane Eyre*, Robert Louis Stevenson's *Treasure Island* and *Kidnapped*, Charles Dickens's *Oliver Twist*, George Orwell's *Animal Farm*, and Alan Paton's *Cry, the Beloved Country*. These changed me; they opened and freed my mind. I still paid attention to politics, however.

Around this time my father wanted me to accept an arranged marriage and come home to be a camel herder, just as the men of our family had always done. I thought I might do that, as I loved camels so, but I wanted to see something of the world first, and I wanted to choose my wife and let her choose me, too. A camel, by the way, can be away from its human family or camel family for twenty years and still know them very well when somehow it comes back. Camels are completely loyal and full of love and courage.

My urge to see something of the larger world was perhaps from all the television and movies and mostly the books. I finished my studies and, giving my apologies to my father, who took me for a walk and said I must learn to take care of my family one way or another if I was to be a man, I headed to Libya to find a good job.

I got there by camel and by truck. Déby, the new president of Chad, was traveling overland to Libya at the same time. He and his motorcade got hopelessly lost in the dunes. Helicopters from Libya found most of them and led them onward. The truck caravan I was in found the rest of his vehicles and gave the men much-needed water. At an oasis, I saw Déby standing and went to greet him and shake his hand.

When you travel across the Sahara by camel, or even by vehicle, it is easy to get lost in the dunes—there are no roads. You just go.

A special red salt, dug from North Darfur, is put in camels' water to help them make the long trip. Horses are of no use here, since it would take three or four camels to carry the water and food needed by one horse. It is better just to take the camels.

If you travel in the summer months, the sun and heat will be very hard on the camels; if you travel in the winter months, the freezing sandstorms will cut your face if you do not hide from them deep in your robes. These are not small trips: you might take your camels a thousand miles, which would be like traveling from Athens to Berlin through all of Serbia, Austria, and the Czech Republic, or from Miami Beach to Philadelphia—a very long way without roads or shelter.

There are many human bones in the desert, particularly where North Darfur blends into the great dunes of the Sahara. Some of these bones are still wearing their clothes and leathery skin, while others have been bleached by hundreds of years of the searing sun. Mirages make birds sitting on distant dunes—birds no bigger than your fist—look like camels. Mirages make dry flatlands look like distant lakes. Mirages make the bones of a single human skeleton look like the buildings of a city far ahead. This sounds impossible, but the Sahara is an impossible place. All trails are erased with each wind. You can note the stars at night, if it is clear, or see where the sun rises or sets, also if it is clear, but it is not always clear, and the tilted horizon provided by the great dunes disorients you even under a cloudless sky. From ten in the morning until about four in the afternoon you cannot guess the direction.

You are modern and think your compass and your GPS will keep you from trouble. But the batteries will give out in your GPS, or the sand will ruin it. Your compass may break or become lost as you try to put away your bedding one morning in a hard sandstorm. So you will want to know the ways that have worked for thousands of years.

If you are good, like my father and brothers, you will put a line of sticks in the sand at night, using the stars to mark your next morning's direction of travel; you can extend this line as needed. Be careful: some people die because they look to a distant mountain as their guide, but the wind moves these mountains around; you might travel in circles until your eyes close and your heart withers.

It says everything about this land to know that even the mountains are not to be trusted, and that the crunching sound under your camel's hooves is usually human bones, hidden and revealed as the wind pleases.

3.
The
Dead Nile

My years away from Darfur were mostly good years. It takes nothing away from them to say that I ended this sojourn as a prisoner in Egypt.

In a prison in Aswan, southern Egypt, a very old jailer—perhaps the age of my own father—was kind enough to let me talk to him through the bars late at night. My Arabic served me well with him, and he asked about my adventures. His company was very welcome.

"Why did you go to Libya? How is it there for a young man like yourself?" he asked as he made a cigarette for himself and one for me.

I told him that I had found a warm community of Zaghawa friends and cousins working along the seacoast there. They made a place for my mattress and found me a restaurant job at a military academy. The Arab students there were also kind to me and lent me their books to study, constantly encouraging me. And always I was asking for more books.

"Ah, you were like the ancient Library of Alexandria once on that shore, demanding the loan of every book from every traveler so it might be copied for the library," he said.

I told him that the library in my head was not quite so good as that, but that I did read about philosophy and history and some politics—and the great novels, of course, which I love and which are read everywhere.

"But you had no passport?"

I told him I did have a visa at first, but I did not have permission to move from Libya to Egypt, where some of my friends had gone and were telling me of much higher wages. Because such workers suffer lonely lives away from home in order to send money to their families, the lure of better pay is very powerful. It is the only thing. So I went to Egypt and worked in restaurants along the Red Sea. I made many friends in Egypt, from every race and background. Then I heard that the wages were even better in Israel. If I could get on the other side of the Red Sea to the Israeli resort town of Eilat, I could go from a hundred dollars a month to about a thousand. This would provide me with enough money to go to college and still send money home. Or perhaps I could find a job in Beersheba, where Ben-Gurion University would be just right for me. I had been working in a restaurant on the Red Sea owned by a Bedouin. I then met a Bedouin man who helped people get across the border to Israel. He showed me where to cross. For me, it was not a good place.

I was immediately captured when I came out of the Gaza Strip into Israel proper. Exhausted, I had fallen asleep by the gushing irrigation pumps of a beautiful farm. I woke to see Israeli soldiers standing around me with their guns pointed at my head.

So I did get to Beersheba, but only to the prison there. It was actually very nice, with television and free international calls. I would recommend it even over many hotels I have known.

I was soon sent back to Egypt, where I was harshly imprisoned. You might have some idea of how bad a prison can be, with the filth and darkness and violence of it, but you would have some ways to go.

"Many die in those Cairo prisons," the old man in Aswan said, but he did not need to tell me that. I had taken my own turn kneeling in the sun all day begging for water and being beaten by the bare fists of a huge guard. I had spent months in a cell so crowded that we had to take turns sitting down. Some of the ninety people in this small room had been there for thirteen years. It was very hot and filled with stench.

A ten-year-old boy was beaten so brutally that he was dying as I tried to comfort him.

How completely sad that he would die so far from his family! In Africa, our families are everything. We do all we can to help them, without question. But I had long known that I could not help my family quite like my brothers did. I could not herd camels and cattle as well as Ahmed, or solve village problems like him; I could not be as hardworking in the bush as Juma, or as patient and good at keeping the family together. For to do such things well requires that they be done happily and forever, and my particular education had inclined me toward a hungry curiosity for the world. But I was not doing so well without my family. *If, if, if I am ever released from this place,* I told myself, *I must return home*—not forever, for that was not my life, but for long enough to heal all the wounds of my long separation.

However, nothing is all bad, and there were many good people to meet in prison from all over Africa with interesting stories for us to listen to as we stood through the nights and days, stepping on roaches and scratching lice but at least getting to learn something interesting about other countries and other people.

After too much of this, the Egyptians were going to send me to Sudan, where, as the old jailer in Aswan advised me, I would probably find my doom. From Aswan, I was going to be put on a Nile boat and taken south to Khartoum.

"It's too bad you could not have stayed in the jail in Israel," the old man said.

Indeed, I agreed, it was a shame to leave.

"If you have some friends, you should get them to try to stop you from being deported to Sudan," he advised.

Some Sudanese men had tried to sneak into Israel from Jordan a few years earlier. After the Israelis sent them back to Jordan, the Jordanians in turn sent them back home to Sudan, where they were executed in Khartoum. This harshness was, I believe, the Arab government of Sudan's way of trying not to be embarrassed in front of other Arab nations regarding its poor economy. When this atrocity was made public by Amnesty International and Human Rights Watch, Israel and other countries agreed not to extradite people to Sudan or to other countries that might do so. When Israel sent me to Egypt, they had Egypt sign an agreement promising not to send me to Sudan. It was happening anyway, unless I could get my situation known to the human rights groups.

Besides this problem, the Egyptian prison had taken a heavy toll on my health, and the old man could see I was very weak. He seemed to have a father's concern. I said that I had no way to contact anyone, and I asked if he could perhaps make a call to my Zaghawa friends in Cairo, who might contact the groups.

"That would be very expensive from here, and I have no money, my son," he said sadly. "Maybe you have some money and I will do it for you."

What happened next was not the first miracle in my life, but it was one of the best. It doesn't matter how many times you put your hands in your empty pockets; when someone asks if you have any money, you will put your hands in there again. This time, after so long in prison, after wearing these old jeans for many months in the vilest of prison cells with nothing to do but stand in the heat and put my hands in my pockets, I somehow let my thumb slip into the tiny watch pocket above the right pocket of my jeans—a forgotten pocket. I felt the edges of something.

Folded into a small square was an Egyptian hundred-pound note, worth maybe twenty U.S. dollars, that I had no memory of ever putting in there. It was tightly folded and frayed after so long, but I unfolded it carefully. It was more than enough for an expensive phone call, certainly.

I gave this to the old man and asked if he would make the phone call for me at a café and perhaps use the rest for a little food for me and for him. Though it was late at night, he returned with a fine chicken dinner for us. He told me details enough of his phone conversation so that I knew he had made the call. Our dinner together reminded me of sharing meals with my father. I had been away from my family a long time, and perhaps that is what I needed to think about in this dark time. My disconnection from them was causing my life great harm. Most of the money was still left, which I gave to the old man for his kindness and because I didn't think there was more than a one percent chance anything could be done for me in time.

My friends in Cairo soon contacted Zaghawa tribal leaders, one as far away as Scandinavia. They in turn contacted Human Rights Watch and the United Nations. Somehow, somehow, somehow, all of that worked. On the day when I had already been sent in chains to a boat on the Nile, and just before the boat began its journey to Khartoum, I was taken off and sent back to Cairo. I would stay in the horrible prison there for a few more months. But then, great miracle, I was allowed to fly away.

It is hard to know where grace comes from. Perhaps the money was always there, waiting for the curiosity that comes with right thinking. For a time, I thought the old jailer had perhaps slipped it in there as I slept. But it was so folded and faded that I think it was waiting for me a long time in that pocket, in the way that many things are waiting for us to be ready to receive them.

4.
A Bad Time
to Go Home

It was the summer of 2003; an Ethiopian Airlines jet lifted me over the Red Sea in late afternoon. My cousins in Britain had purchased my ticket home. The plane banked over the Nile and then floated south above the river with a view west into the Sahara. Almost as if I had died in the Egyptian prison and was now going home on the wind, there was a magic-carpet feeling to it. I could see, for the first time in my life, the immensity of the Sahara: a forever sea of sand below with scattered dots of green, with the curled and weathered backbones of dead mountains, with the chalk threads of camel trails and dry streams tracing delicate currents around the dunes.

As we continued to rise, the trails disappeared and the dunes became the rough weave of a canvas extending to the distant horizon. This desert of sand is about the size of the entire United States. From above, it is easy to understand why men must build great pyramids to achieve any notice here. *Amazing to be alive and see such things,* I thought as I rested my head beside the window and sipped a tea. I watched a red sunset spill over the land. *Amazing to be alive. Humdallah, humdallah, amazing. God bless my cousins in London. God bless my friends in Cairo and the human rights groups. God bless the old jailer in Aswan. God bless the hundred-pound note in my jeans. God please even bless the person who invented those little pockets in jeans where such a note might become long lost and someday found. God bless Ahmed and all my brothers and sisters and my mother and father.*

After so many years away, I would see them all soon, though they were now, as my cousins informed me, in the middle of a war. My brother Ahmed would be happiest to see me, and would want to know everything of my adventures. *God bless Ahmed.* I could see him already in front of me, delighted to hear each turn of my story.

In the distance somewhere just beyond my view to the west was Khartoum, its lights probably just now blinking on, the blue dusk probably shining in the strands of the Nile River where it is born from the White and Blue Niles. The Blue comes from Ethiopia and contributes the most water, while the White comes a far greater distance through Lake Victoria, losing much of its water in the vast swamps of southern Sudan. In ancient times there was another great river in Sudan, running through Darfur west to Lake Chad. The great valley where it once ran is the Wadi Howar, also called the Dead Nile by the people. Except for the summer rain time, its waters now flow under the sand.

After a stop in Addis Ababa, I flew in a southern loop through Kenya, Uganda, and the Central African Republic, then cut back up across South Darfur in Sudan. Mostly it was dark below, as most of this land has little or no electricity and goes to bed early. The stars and a new moon were all I could see for most of this time, until suddenly there were some flickering lights below.

"Where are we?" I asked the young flight attendant whom I had come to know a little; she was perhaps my age, about thirty. She leaned over to look out my window, letting her hand rest gracefully on my shoulder for balance.

"Nowhere, I think!" she smiled as she looked patiently into the dark.

By asking the time until landing, I calculated that we were probably crossing over southern Sudan and very probably South Darfur. The lights below were likely the lights of war—the last flaring of huts and villages attacked earlier that day, of great, centuries-old village trees that had become like bonfires. Darfur was burning.

I rubbed the Zaghawa scars on my temple as I looked down at this dark scene. Somewhere down there—though north of there, really—were my friends, my mother and my father, my sisters and my brothers, uncountable cousins, aunts, uncles, our camels, donkeys, our songbirds, our thousand years of stories. You can imagine this for yourself, friend, flying home and seeing your homeland below in points of fire. Whatever warrior blood comes to you from your ancestors would be working inside you.

Yet, perhaps because I had already seen something of the larger world, it was not so simple as that; I was indeed observing from this altitude. I counted among my friends the people of many tribes and many races, and this makes a difference in our hearts. I counted also among my acquaintances Jane Eyre, Long John Silver, and Oliver Twist.

Altitude itself is a powerful thing. When travelers are in space, looking at our small planet from a distance where borders and flags cannot be seen or imagined, this also, I am told, bends one toward a peaceful view. That is what I wanted, really, just peace. I was sad and anxious for my people but not angry. I didn't want to kill any human person. I didn't even hate the man who was organizing all these crimes, the president of Sudan, though I wished deeply to take him for a long walk through the villages of my childhood and perhaps change his way of thinking about how best to serve the people, which is surely his job.

We floated in the predawn over the deserts of Chad, descending finally into the oasis of N'Djamena (you just say it "Jameena"). Here I had friends and cousins who would give me a place to sleep. With a few dollars from my cousins, I could cross Chad and slip into Darfur in a remote place unnoticed by the Sudan government.

The stairway rolled up to the plane a little after 5 A.M. in N'Djamena. Last off, I paused for a moment atop the stairs; the moist smell of the river, the great starry sky of my freedom greeted me—*Humdallah, humdallah, the Africa of my friends and my family!*

From this small porch I could see, even at this early hour, Chadian military vehicles and aircraft moving around the base beside the small airport. The city, too, was already awake with its normal business and the added seasoning of war's excitement.

The body responds to this. The smells and sounds, the movements of soldiers and vehicles, are all taken in quickly with the keener perceptions that awaken in dangerous times.

Some cousins were at the airport and I was soon eating a wonderful breakfast: kebab meats in rich, very spicy sauces. The news of the war in neighboring Sudan surrounded me: news from cousins here and there in North Darfur; news learned from cell phones and passing travelers; news about villages attacked here, of deaths in the family there, of cousins taking arms to defend their villages, of sisters missing and mothers killed or raped. There was a great sadness and also a great excitement everywhere: our great nest of bees had been swatted hard.

After several days to recover my health, I told my eldest cousin that it was time for me to go to Darfur. He shook my hand and held my shoulder as if he would not see me again. I was given the money I would need for fares in the Land Cruisers that string together the villages of Africa. The women of the family wrapped some food for me to take. I went to a marketplace and found a ride in what looked like a good Land Cruiser with a good driver.

Packed shoulder to shoulder with other travelers, I was soon heading across the rain-flooded wadis.

The Darfur regions of Sudan are on Chad's eastern border, about six hundred miles and two days away from N'Djamena on bad roads. We stopped in village marketplaces where some riders would leave and others would pile in. The newer riders bore the ceremonial scars of the Zaghawa, my own people. From these people I learned of the troubles ahead: the burned villages, the rush of people across the border into Chad from Darfur. My stomach hurt with fear for my family.

Everyone knows the family of everyone else among the Zaghawa. If you live in a small town, you know a great deal about the families who live there. If your town had no television or other things to take you away from visiting all the time, your town could be very large and you would still know something about everyone. So it is like that. And of course when people travel close together like this on long journeys, you get to know a great deal about many people. Everyone is well-known eventually.

We finally arrived in the sprawling mud-brick, tin-roof city of Abéché, the last big community in Chad before the Sudan border. It is home to sixty or seventy thousand people in peaceful times, but now was thick with refugees and Chadian soldiers arriving to control the long border and prevent trouble. The soldiers let the refugees come across from Darfur since it was the only humane thing that could be done, and because there is a tradition of hospitality that prevents you from turning away your visitors.

In Abéché I found a ride for the last, but very rough, ten miles to the Sudan border, to the town of Tine. I had been able to get very little sleep so far. Tine would be a good place to rest.

As we approached the town, the smell found us before we could see any huts. It was the smell of tea brewing and food cooking. Tine is Zaghawa, so the cooking smells were very nice after such a long time away.

I went to the sultan's home, a fenced enclosure of several large huts. All visitors there are always welcomed with a mattress to sleep outdoors in the enclosure and with good food, for the sultan is there to care for the people.

The war was bringing people by the thousands to the sultan, who was asking his omdas, who look out for the several regions of his kingdom, and his sheikhs, who look out for one village each, to arrange hospitality for the refugees. In North Darfur, for example, there are five such sultans. Several more are in West Darfur, several more in South Darfur, and several more, like this one, in Chad. These compose the ancient nation of Darfur, and Darfur is still organized as it was in the 1500s. The sultanships are hereditary, while the omdas and the sheikhs are appointed by the sultan because they have earned the respect of the people they live among. It is a very different kind of democracy, with the people voting for their local leaders not with ballots, but rather with their attitudes of respect for those who stand out in their service to their communities. The tally is kept in the mind of the sultan. At the national level, of course, there are regular elections, though they are now so corrupted by Bashir that they have no power to reflect the will and wisdom of the people.

The sultan shook my hand and held my shoulder when we first met.

"How is your father and your brother Ahmed?" he asked me. When he said this with such respect, I knew Ahmed would someday be the sheikh of our village.

He told me that I had some cousins who, having fled Darfur, were now living in Tine, and he told me exactly where they could be found. He welcomed me to stay as long as I pleased, then went back to the thousand emergencies pressing down on him.

Some of the arriving people were gravely wounded by bombs and bullets in the attacks on their villages across the border. Some of the children who had come a long way were thin and ill. Some of the women and girls had been raped and were seriously injured by that. Family members were searching from village to village to find one another, and the sultan, omdas, and sheikhs were helping to find these people and take care of everyone.

Amid all this rush of people and trouble, I lay down on the ground to rest. Because it had rained, plastic tarps were put down under the mattresses provided to guests. Despite the constant coming and going of people and the crying of children, I fell deeply asleep.

In the morning, after drinking green tea with many others, I went looking for a Land Cruiser that would be heading north to Bahai, which is forty-five miles up the border and a good place to cross into Darfur without notice.

In the Tine marketplace, men were cleaning their guns—mostly old rifles and Kalashnikovs—and talking about where they might be most useful. They were buying and trading ammunition and supplies. Others, without guns, were also organizing to go back into Darfur to find relatives and friends. That, of course, was my situation, and I was soon on the road.

As we traveled, we could look to our right across the great valley separating Chad from Sudan and see the white bombers and helicopters in the distance. These aircraft were bombing villages. We saw funnels of smoke against the horizon. We saw Janjaweed militia units moving down in the wadi, not far from us.

Bahai, my last stop in Chad, was finally in view. It is a small town of scattered huts and mud-brick stores on the flats near a river crossing. Because it is a different Zaghawa kingdom than Tine, there is a different sultan in the area. I paid my respects to him. Like the sultan in Tine, this one was also surrounded by many people who had crowded over the river. And as in Tine, the town was filled with families seeking their lost members, with wounded men, women, and children seeking care. Vacant-eyed people, shocked by the sudden loss of their homes and families, were walking everywhere. Groups of armed defenders were organizing everywhere.

I paid a driver and pulled myself up into the back of the next truck heading deep into Darfur.

We crossed the river against a current of people escaping. All along the muddy roads and along the flats where every vehicle makes its own road, we passed refugees walking toward Chad. We encouraged them as we passed, telling them that safety was only a mile farther, then only two miles farther, only a half day farther, and soon we would only say that they were walking the right way. We gave much of our water to mothers and children.

The white Antonov bombers were visible from time to time, and smoke was often seen rising behind the hills. Village defenders and other resistance fighters sometimes stopped us on the road. Our trucks were white, as are any civilian Land Cruisers or other trucks that might otherwise be mistaken for military vehicles. Even so, the resistance fighters reminded us that the helicopters and bombers would not care about such things. So every turn of our journey was carefully traveled, our eyes watching the sky and the distant hills and wadis. We would lean out and look at the tire tracks beside the road to know who had come this way and that. Fresh tracks from big tires would mean government trucks and death. Fresh horse tracks in great numbers would mean Janjaweed and death. This constant observation was a good travel activity to help pass the hours, as our situation was truly in God's hands, not our own.

When, in the trance and bounce of the long journey, I would think of the whole situation, it did seem like a bad dream. This part of the world, our world, was changing so quickly every day, falling deeper into the fires of cruelty. I wanted to wake up from it. Imagine if all the systems and rules that held your country together fell apart suddenly and your family members were all—every one of them— in a dangerous situation. It was like that. You cannot be thinking of yourself at such a time; you are making calculations of where your friends and family members might be, and where they might go. You are recalculating this con-stantly, deciding what you might do to help them.

5.

My Sister's
Village

I had decided even before leaving Egypt that I would go first to my older sister's village, so I would then have some news about her to give my mother and father in our own village.

After some rough mountains, the approach into her village was along a dry river. Wells and small pools—the water points of the village—were pocked with bomb craters. The normal rush of village children toward a visiting vehicle was absent. The outlying clusters of huts were burned, though some had mud rooms and enclosures that were still standing.

I had been to this village many times, including for several weddings, which are a big part of life for us. A wedding goes on for four evenings, with wonderful dancing and singing. I saw an area of large trees and remembered all the dancing that used to happen under them. The women form a long line and sing traditional songs about village life, and then dance in this long line—so beautiful in their brightly colored gowns floating about them in the firelight. The men watch and jump in a ceremonial way. In ancient days they would have their spears with them, since this was the symbol of the male. At the last wedding I went to, some men had guns and they fired them in the air, to show their appreciation for the great dancing and singing by the women.

That now seemed so long ago, and forever lost. As we arrived, we could see that many huts were still standing. My sister's hut was among them.

After my sister Halima recovered from seeing the man her baby brother had grown to be, she made a small joke that I was always doing things backward, that a Hari should not come home to roost in the middle of a war. She was joking that our family name, *Hari,* means "eagle." Birds are famous for leaving a village before a battle, not for arriving during one.

Her husband was away somewhere with a group of men. They were perhaps moving the animals to safety or preparing to defend the village. Women are often not told about the troubles of war, though they suffer them greatly.

But whether they are told or not, the women know everything. The children see it all and, as they do their chores, the women ask them to tell what they have seen. I did not ask Halima where my brother-in-law might be. He was somewhere doing what needed doing, just as the women were busy hiding caches of food out in the wadis to the west of the village, should a hasty escape be necessary.

Halima told me of the prior bombings in the village,

which killed seven people. I knew these families, though some of the victims had come into the world in the years I was away. Thus I had missed their whole lives, which was very sad to me.

In the evening, when the children of the village finished their chores with the animals and gardens, I talked to them under a tree in a slight rain.

"Tell me what happened," I asked the eldest boy, who was perhaps fourteen and would surely be among the resistance troops in a few days or weeks. He was wearing torn jeans and a shredded UCLA sweatshirt that probably had come through marketplaces from Algeria to El Fasher, having first been donated years ago in the United States.

"All the birds flew up and away. This is the first thing we noticed," he said.

Then he mimicked the noise of the Antonov bomber as it cruised high over the village.

"We could not see it," he said. The others nodded.

"But our mothers knew it was the Antonov as soon as they saw the birds leave, and they yelled at us to go hide in the wadi, and take some animals quickly. So we took the donkeys and some chickens and goats as fast as we could. As we ran, we could hear people in the village yelling to get this person or that person out of a hut and help them get away. We could not hear the Antonov at this time. We thought it had gone away and we were safe, and that our mothers were crazy. Our fathers were far away with the animals.

"Then we heard the Antonov coming back," the boy continued under the tree. "It was coming lower, and we could see it coming up the wadi. It dropped a big bomb on each of the water points along the wadi to destroy the wells and maybe to poison them with this . . ."

The boy then pulled up his sleeve to show me red blisters on his arm. Other boys did the same, revealing backs, necks, legs, and stomachs burned by some chemical.

"The bombs sent balls of fire and sharp metal everywhere, even to where we were hiding, where the metal came down like rain—*ting, ting, ting, ting*—for a long time. Some trees and huts were on fire when we came running back to find our mothers and grandparents."

I noticed how loud the boys were talking, and then I realized they were not hearing well. I remembered how the RPGs had damaged my own hearing for a long time when I was a little boy caught in an attack.

Seven people were dead, but the toll could have been much worse if not for the vigilance of the women. It could have been much worse if helicopter gunships had chased down the children and women, as happened so many other places. It could have been worse if the attack had been followed by the armed horsemen of the Janjaweed and the government's own troops, who would have raped every girl and woman and then shot everyone they could find. This had not happened yet to this village, but they understood it was yet to come.

Many dead animals still needed to be buried or taken away. I tended to some of this, helping wherever I could.

The smell of the chemical was still heavy on the village. It made everyone, especially the children, suffer diarrhea and vomiting for several days. Many had difficulty breathing, particularly the very young and old. The birds who drank from the water points began to die. Fifty or more camels and other animals who had trusted the water too soon lay dead at the wells.

Junked appliances and other scrap metal had been packed around the huge bombs dropped by the Sudanese government, creating a million flying daggers with each explosion. I had heard that this was happening, but did not believe it until I saw the pieces of junk stuck in the trunks of trees. Most of those killed by the bombs were buried in several pieces.

The women, normally dressed in bright colors or in the white robes of mourning, were now all in dark browns to make themselves less visible in the desert. They had poured sand in their hair, which is a custom of grieving for the dead, and they began to look like the earth itself. The children were in the darkest colors their mothers could find for them. All the bright color of the village, except a sad sprinkling of dead songbirds, was now gone.

After the second day I told Halima that it was time for me to go find our parents and the others of our family in the home village. We said goodbye very warmly, because we well knew the trouble coming.

6.
The End
of the
World

There is a small town within a few hours' walk of my home village. Like most towns in the middle of an area of villages, it has a marketplace and a boys' school and a girls' school, all with mud-brick buildings.

As we approached the town in the Land Cruiser, we moved from the flat desert into a wadi between small mountains. We drove along the sand of the dry riverbed. Up ahead would be, in normal times, green trees, the sound of birds, and the smell of cooking. Boys and girls would be tending animals at the water points along the sandy bottom. All that was different now. Many of the trees were now burned and the water points were blackened and cratered. There were very few birds.

The children of the village looked at us seriously instead of running along beside us. Their animals were nowhere to be seen. Some burned huts were still smoking.

Each family compound has a kitchen hut that usually includes three or four red clay vessels inside, called *nunus*, full of millet. These are sometimes much bigger than you can reach around, and can be fairly squat or as tall as a man. These silos can keep millet for ten or fifteen years and provide some insurance for hard times. From the burned huts, the smoke from these vessels layered the village with a smell of burned cooking, plus the burnt-hair smell of smoldering blankets and mattresses. There was also the smell of the dead, since not every animal had been buried yet.

I went first to the sheikh's huts: I knew him well and so could get the best information there. His huts were partially burned; no doubt everyone had rushed to help put out the fire here, since the sheikh's house is everyone's house. There was a busy coming and going of people now. Burials were being arranged and some of the wounded were being tended to. I was told who was dying over in that family and who over in this family, so that I could visit them before they died. There are no doctors or medicines in these villages, so you will die if you are seriously wounded. You bear your pain as bravely as possible and pray for death to come. Your people come to be with you. I knew everyone except the children in this village, so I visited the seventeen badly wounded people who were dying. Some had lost arms or legs in the explosions or had great wounds loosely held together with stitches of wool thread or animal hair. The only medicine or pain relief was a cup of tea.

These were people I had grown up with and played games with under the moon—we played games at night because we were busy with chores in the day, and the daytime heat was too much.

I visited a young woman whom I had always admired when we played together. She had been so strong and joyful. It was not proper for me to hold her hand, though I longed to do so now. Maybe you can think of who this would be if this happened in your hometown, and you may know how I was feeling.

Two days before my arrival the seven water points of the village had been hit with large bombs, and this had set some of the huts afire. It had not been the first attack. Each day now, the children were sent away from the village. The animals were brought to the few usable water points late at night for watering. In the daytime, anything moving in the village would invite bombs or helicopter attacks. Still, no ground attack had come.

Every cousin I met told me of ten or more deaths in his part of the family. All the villages to the east were under attack, and the men in this village were preparing for what might come next. The women were tending the wounded and were preparing food and supplies to hide in the wadis and pack on the donkeys.

While some men were organized to wait in place and defend the villages, others joined resistance groups that roamed in vehicles to be wherever they could be of most use. The government was attacking so many villages at once that these men were stretched thin and exhausted. The five kingdoms of North Darfur—Dar Kobe, Dar Gala, Dar Artaj, Dar Sueni, and our own Dar Tuar—were all under attack at the same time. Kingdoms in West and

South Darfur were also being hit. The resistance fighters—some barely fourteen years old—would come into the villages in pieced-together Land Rovers for water and food, then would speed away to the next emergency, leaving their wounded with the women of the village. While the kingdom's system of sultans, omdas, and sheikhs was until recently a superbly efficient form of military organization, no one was giving orders now; the facts of each new day overwhelmed all plans.

I was told by the sheikh that my own smaller village had been bombed once but was not badly damaged, and that my immediate family was not harmed. Knowing this, I stayed in the larger village a few days to help where I could. There was a great movement of refugees through this town and people needed every kind of assistance.

Many men were joining resistance groups; you would see very young teenage boys jumping into the backs of trucks with a family weapon and that was it for them. No one in the boys' families would try to stop them. It was as if everybody had accepted that we were all going to die, and it was for each to decide how they wanted to go. It was like that. The end of the world was upon us.

"We are leaving now to try to get to Chad," was the anthem of many families as they moved through the sheikh's compound to say their goodbyes. They received advice as to the best ways through the mountains and wide deserts. Chad was far away. Even if they were not attacked by troops or Janjaweed or helicopters, many would not survive the hundred-mile trip through the scorching desert. The rain time would be over in a few days, after which the desert would dry very quickly. But there were not many other choices. Some said they would hide in local wadis and wait for peace. And there are caves in the mountains, as I well knew. But most people were intent on finding safety in Chad, where Zaghawa relatives would take care of them until they could return. Below all these adult conversations gazed the worried eyes of silent children. And in every adult eye was the dullness of a fatal understanding: whatever we do, our world is now ending and we commend ourselves into God's rough or gentle Hands.

"Your home village will soon be attacked," the sheikh told me as we stood together after tea, watching his people go. He kept track of where the refugees were coming from; he knew where the lines of attack were spreading. So I bid him goodbye and thanked him for his lifetime of courtesies to my family and to me. He said that he had always been honored to serve us; he bid me give his greetings to my father and my mother and to Ahmed and my sister, all of whom he respected greatly.

I climbed aboard a Land Cruiser loaded with guns and men headed in the direction of my own small village. There was not much conversation as we bounced quickly through the wadis. There ahead, in a lovely nest of green, was my home village. I stepped off within sight of my family's huts and said goodbye for the last time to these fellows in the vehicle.

"See you soon, Daoud," said an old school friend with a serious smile, meaning *not in this lifetime.*

7.

Homecoming

It was not the homecoming I had longed for after these years away. I was not returning with gifts and money for everyone.

"Daoud is returned," I heard some men say as I walked by groups that were gathered here and there. I nodded to them but it did not seem to be a time for smiles and joyful greetings.

I walked into the family enclosure where a donkey, several goats, and some chickens watched my arrival. My father was on the far side of the village with some other men, as were my brothers. I saw my mother under the shade roof attached to the cooking hut; she was with my sister Aysha and with several other women of the village; they were all in mourning. Mother looked very old now. Her hair was matted with the earth of grieving. She wore dark clothing, a dark shawl over her old head. She saw me and wept into her hands, as if it were even sadder for her to think that my homecoming had to be at such a time.

"*Fatah*," she managed to say, which is what you say when you greet someone in a time of grieving.

"Fatah," I replied. I stood a distance away from her. We did not touch or embrace, following the custom. She would try to say something, but then begin to cry again into her hands and her shawl. We had lost perhaps twenty cousins in the previous days, and each was like a son or daughter to her. In tribal life, cousins are as close as brothers and sisters and, in such times of loss, it physically hurts. In this tiny village, three children and their mother were killed when the white Antonov bomber came. Six of the fifty houses were burned. This news, which I already knew, was told to me again by the women as I stood with my head bowed a little to my mother.

They recounted the deaths of each person: how it happened, what was happening to that family, and good things to remember about each person. It is good to remember the dead at such times, for soon, after the period of mourning, any photo and reminder of that person will be removed. The person's clothes will be given away to a distant village. The past is past. There is too much death in the land of no doctors for it to be any other way.

I heard running and then saw Ahmed come through the enclosure. He was, against the mourning custom and his own intentions, smiling somewhat as he grasped my arm in a great handshake.

"Daoud," he said. "Fatah. So it's all true—you have come back."

"Fatah," I replied, trying not to smile also.

He took me into the sun, away from the low voices of the women. He knew of all my adventures, every detail of every job and every jail, every narrow escape. It was crazy of me to think I would have anything to tell him. The goats and the family donkey came up to nuzzle him as he spoke.

Ahmed looked older but excellent. He now took care of several entire families whose men had died.

"Let me take you to Father," he said after our brief visit. I gave my greetings again to my mother and my sister and the other women, and he led me out into the village, his long arm draped over my shoulders.

In this I felt at home. I had been feeling like a visitor in Darfur, even in my old village—like someone from another world. But Ahmed's arm on my shoulder was the gentleness of home.

"It's very, very good to see you, Daoud," he said several times. I told him that the sheikh had sent his regards and had warned of an attack soon.

"Yes, an attack I think will come in a few days," Ahmed said. "Not tomorrow, but maybe soon after that. We are almost ready to move the people out. You can help get some people ready, if you want to do that," he said.

"Of course," I answered.

We approached a group of old men talking under an old tree.

"Fatah," I said to the eldest of them, my father. He was in his eighties, which is unusually old for this land. He stood with the help of his herding stick, opened his arms, and gave me a long embrace.

"Fatah," father whispered into my hair. "So, you have come back from all your adventures," he said. "We have learned much of the world and its prisons from following the news about you," he chided me in good humor.

"Praise heaven you are home safely, but I think you have come just in time for some more trouble for you," he added. "May God keep you safe."

The other men stood to shake my hand and embrace me. We visited an hour before I went to look for Ahmed, who had escaped the old men to continue his preparations. I found him in front of his family enclosure, talking to more than twenty men, mostly thirty-five to forty-five years old. They were planning to move the old people and young children in the next two days. Because they also talked about preparing their guns, I later asked Ahmed what this group was going to do.

"We are the village defenders," he said. "We will stay behind to slow the attack if it comes before everyone has left. It is what we are trained to do, and you are not."

He told me that most of the younger men had already gone to the rebel groups. There were other defenders in the mountains from other villages who would come when they were called.

In the old days, the sultan of an area had a great war drum. Actually, some of these drums still exist. They are so big that ten men can beat them with great clubs. The sound of this drum—I heard it more than once as a child—will carry over the desert the distance of a two- or three-day walk. In the rain time, when there are low clouds, it will carry even farther. In this way, all the villages in the sultan's reach would know that there is a sad problem that must be solved with fighting. The sultan would send representatives to the omdas, and the village sheiks would go to the omdas to get the news and learn the strategy. Perhaps, for example, Arabs had stolen some cattle and would not pay. There was no higher court to take the problem to, so there would be a battle at some agreed-upon field of honor. As I have said, it would be far away from the women and children.

We boys would have to go find the strongest of the male camels so that our fathers and older brothers would have good mounts for the battle. Guns and swords would swing from their saddles as they left the village without a word of information or consolation to the children or women. The camels would know what all this meant, and they would grind their teeth in a way that could be heard all over the village. The sound of worried camels was the sound before battle, while the ululation of wailing women was the sound after the battle. The names of the fallen would arrive long before the weary camels and men plodded back into the village. The surviving men would split up and spend up to two weeks in the family enclosures of the widows, so that the women would have company and could overhear their stories. This was how their lost husbands were honored. In time, the widow might be taken as an extra wife by one of her late husband's brothers or another man.

I tell you all this because I was hearing again the grinding sound of worried camels, and the birds flew up and down as if they were unsure of which place might be safe.

Over dinner, Ahmed reminded me of all the paths

through the wadi, of all the water points in remote places, and of our childhood caves.

"It will not be easy for all these people to get quickly away," he said. "Men like you, who tended animals so far into the desert when they were boys, could, if they chose, help them find their way." He was not inviting me to go, but he was clearly not inviting me to stay and die—and I had no gun. Ahmed was thinking clearly. He had sent another of our brothers to El Fasher, the safest town in North Darfur, as a kind of family insurance: no matter what happened, there would be one alive to help the surviving women and children of the family. There was no way for all the family to go with him, as there were too many animals to tend.

We ate chicken that evening and the next several evenings—wonderful chicken, usually saved for special occasions. Everyone in the village ate chicken those nights.

I borrowed *jallabiya* robes to wear from Ahmed. I had not been in the flowing clothes for many years, but it was pleasant to wear them now—they were cooler in the sun than my Western khakis. They bring you shade wherever you go. I borrowed one of Ahmed's camels and checked on the animals at the water points. I used the camel whip very lightly to get some speed along the sand. I saw a shadow in the sand of who I might have been had I stayed.

I was happy to find my place again in my big and loving family. Maybe Heaven is like this, a warm reunion of those you love after dark times and a long separation, but with a little excitement to keep things interesting.

Ahmed told me that some of the old people were refus-
ing to leave. They were intent on dying where they had always lived. They would not be humiliated and made to run
away from their homes.

I asked about our parents. Ahmed was planning to get
them out soon. They were willing to go.

Some families had already left. A few of these had
arranged vehicle rides to other villages, but most had children and animals and belongings, and would have to walk.

Our family's animals, like those of most families, were
in faraway places known only to us.

I spent the days helping people get ready. I would ride
to the outlying clusters of huts and encourage people to
prepare to move. Some did not want to, and would point
and say, "We have our great-grandfathers buried over here,
and our children buried over there, and so why would this
not be a good place for us to die also?" You could not argue
with that. This meant we had to think about the women
and children and the younger men and help them instead.

Women were getting their children ready for the long
journey, and you may know what this is like, though it was
probably more serious in this kind of situation. What to
take, what to leave—all those difficult choices.

I woke up late one night with a vivid dream. Ahmed
was standing in the middle of the village. Two of his fellow
village defenders were near him, screaming for him to run.
I was shouting down to them from the hillside, telling
them to shoot at the attackers. *Don't yell at Ahmed,* I shouted,
shoot the attackers over there, over there, and I pointed because I
could see them taking aim at Ahmed. But it was too late,

and Ahmed fell from a bullet. *Why didn't you shoot the attackers?*
I shouted when I got down to the men. *Why didn't you shoot
them?* But Ahmed was dead, and then maybe I was dead.

This dream kept me awake. I walked out of the village
to the hill beside it. I was still up there in the bushes at
dawn.

I had tea for breakfast at my father's hut. (Husbands
and wives have separate huts, which makes for long mar-
riages.) Ahmed was there and I looked at him like he was a
dead man. I could not tell him the dream. Ahmed was
telling my father to leave the village right after tea, and to
take the rest of the animals out of the village. My father,
who said he had heard guns in the night, agreed and left.

At about 9 A.M. I was walking through the village to see
how everyone was doing. It was a morning of good weather
at the end of the rain time. The birds were singing, which I
took to mean we were safe at least another hour. But then
there was a strange sound and I stopped walking in order
to listen carefully. It was a thumping like a great drum, then
more and very rapid thumps of this drum. Then very
clearly it was the sound of helicopters turning steeply. I saw
two large, green helicopters now through the trees, turning
sharply into our narrow wadi. The thumping was their engines as they turned—then the thumping of their guns
shook the air. I did not know which way to run so I stood
there crazy for a moment and watched the dirt of the village spraying up from the bullets.

I saw Ahmed run from his enclosure with his gun. My
other brother, Juma, was with him. Juma is a quiet, very
hardworking man. I was not used to seeing him excited and

with a gun. Juma and Ahmed seemed now to be running to the sound of this drumming. They were headed to the mouth of the little valley where the ground attackers would have to enter. Their running also drew the helicopters away from the huts. Other defenders were now running up to the hills on both sides of the village, but mostly to the east to intercept the attackers as far down the valley as they could manage.

"Let's go! Let's go!" they shouted to one another over the steady *kata-tata* of the machine guns.

The women started screaming to their children *Let's go let's go* and everything in the village began to move in a swirl of dust and noise. The animals were wild-eyed with fear, and the donkeys screamed and brayed. I did not see where the bullets were going, but little songbirds flew down from the trees, confused and worried. They perched on my shoulders and then hid in the folds of my robes and shawl. But then I saw they were falling dead from me, their hearts broken by this noise. I ran to my mother's hut. She and my sister and her children were already leaving, quickly moving between the huts to the safety of the trees and the rocky wadi west of the village. *Let's go let's go,* she called to her grandbabies as they ran toward the safety of the trees and the steep rocks to the west of the village. I quickly found myself with other men carrying a child here, boosting some children onto donkeys, urging donkeys along *let's go let's go,* finding children and sometimes their mothers standing and crying hysterically and pleading with them to move along.

"You can cry, but you must move also, *let's go*. You must

get your children behind those trees and keep going—go, go, go!"

One hundred people had wisely left the village in the days before the attack; we were now struggling with the one hundred and fifty remaining. The older people willing to go needed the most help; we were constantly coming back to help this person and again for the next person, with the bullets cracking in the trees and RPG rounds exploding in the center of the village and setting huts on fire. We were checking flaming huts and carrying the people who could not run. There was a sort of slow dreaminess to all this.

I am dead, I am dead, this is how I died, it is not so bad, I was thinking, afraid to look down at my body because too many bullets were flying around for me still to be okay. I kept moving, moving, carrying the people to the trees and up into the rocky ravine, looking back and hoping to see no one else needing help, but seeing them and going back.

The small, camouflage-painted Land Cruisers of the attackers were now visible at the lower part of the village. The defenders had moved quickly enough to pin them in place and buy us this time. Defenders from other villages nearby had heard the helicopters and were coming over the hills to help. The Sudanese Army troops and the Janjaweed are cruel but they are not stupid, and they did not rush into this little valley so quickly and become trapped; the defenders had thought this out very well.

Large-caliber machine guns were firing into the village from far enough away that attackers could only spray the area and hope to kill people without seeing them. The helicopters were mostly shooting at the defenders at the east end and not at the people escaping to the west. They would all surely come after us when the defenders were dead, so we knew we had to keep moving.

This pushing of the people into the mountains went on for perhaps fifteen or twenty minutes, though it seemed like many hours. You have to keep going, keep going, up steep places and onward to places where Janjaweed horsemen would not be able to follow.

I could see, as we moved the last of the people out of the village, the Janjaweed now charging in on their horses, shooting into the huts as they came. We had everyone but the defenders out by this time. We slipped into the rocks and watched from above for a moment before we continued on, pushing at the rear of this exodus to keep it going.

Being ready to go had worked a great miracle, as all but the defenders were now safely out of the village. I looked behind me, far down to the sand, and could see no children's bodies, no women's bodies, on the sand or between the huts or trees. A very good view, under my circumstances.

Behind us, the defenders held down the attackers and we heard their firing dwindle over the hour. Finally it was silent. We kept moving through all that day and all that night. The fast march was hardest on the children and on the old who had chosen to come, but the great fear now was that the helicopters would come looking for us, as they often did after an attack.

People cried as they walked, thinking of what they had

left behind, and they cried for the defenders and some of
the old people who had stayed.

We could settle down some of the boys by saying, *Someday you will have this great story to tell your children.* There was
nothing, however, that could be said to the young girls and
the women, who could not see the future anymore. Our
village was gone. Some of the best of our men were dead.
There was no reason not to cry as they walked in several
dark lines through the mountain.

The surviving village defenders caught up with us toward dark. My brother Juma was among them, but I did
not see Ahmed with him. Juma looked at me sadly when he
came closer. This was enough.

"Fatah," he said. "Our brother Ahmed is killed. Maybe
we will see him soon."

We held each other. He told me that the badly wounded
were staying about three hours back on the trail so the
women and children would not see them. It is considered
impolite for a man, whose job is to be strong, to present
himself to women or children when he is badly hurt.

I had thought in my heart that Ahmed and Juma
were probably dead. Seeing Juma alive was very good, but
Ahmed's death hit me very hard now. We would have to
tell Mother and our sister. It might be too much for them.

They stood and listened as Juma and I told them. They
appealed to their God for strength that starry night.

In the morning, and the next morning, we could hear
bombing and helicopters in the distance; other villages
were dying.

On the third day of our flight we came to a water point where some of our people were waiting for us, including Father. He had some of our camels and other animals in his care. He already knew about Ahmed and looked much older on account of this news.

Fifteen of us, the younger men, decided to ride camels back to the village to bury the dead and retrieve the hidden supplies of food and clothing. The attackers would have taken all they wanted by now, burned the village, and gone away. We needed to bury the bodies before the wild dogs and jackals destroyed them. We gathered some tools for burial and rode back.

The village was mostly gone—sixty or so scorched black spots where a whole world once celebrated life. The nunus of millet, many mattresses and blankets, mounds of trees, and parts of huts were still smoking, which we smelled long before we entered the wadi.

Thirteen bodies were on the ground, mostly near the eastern side of the village, where the defense was made. The Sudanese troops and Janjaweed had of course removed their own dead, so these thirteen were the defenders of the village and some who had come to help.

I found Ahmed. The effects of large-caliber weapons and perhaps an RPG round were such that I barely recognized his body, but it was Ahmed. I dug a grave as we do, so that he would rest on his right side with his face to the east. I put the pieces of this great fellow in the deep sand forever.

"Goodbye, Ahmed," I said to him. And I knelt down there for a long time instead of helping the others. It was raining a little.

Finally, I did stand and go help the others.

After we retrieved some hidden supplies and packed them on our camels, we prepared to leave. Mixed deep in the ashes of the smoldering huts were of course the bones of the old people who had refused to go, but we could do nothing for these now until the rains would reveal them. The wild animals would have no use for these fired bones.

A few birds were singing in the trees. Not many, but a few. *Well,* I thought to myself, *they will come back in time, like the people.*

But for now it was ashes and graves. This had been a good village.

8.
The
Seven
of Us

When we caught up with our people we men stayed mostly together with the wounded defenders, going back and forth to the women for the food and for the traditional medicine and teas they would prepare. In this way our village, though now a moving line in the desert, was still the same people helping one another.

The people of other villages joined us here and there, until we were a great mass of people moving across the land. Every morning we would have to bury several of the wounded who died in the night. It was good for some of them to die, since there was no morphine or other medicine. You can usually see in a man's eyes if he will be blessed to die before morning.

On the fifth day we came to a remote and grassy valley, and some of those with animals to sustain them decided they would hide there and make a temporary life. Those with no animals had no choice but to continue on to Chad.

My mother and sister were among these who stayed—she would go no farther. My father would keep moving with some of the animals and the other people while they needed him. The camels provided wonderful milk and rides for the children, who were suffering. He would come back to Mother with our animals when he could. In this way, my mother and sister became what the world calls IDPs, which means internally displaced persons—refugees who are still within their home country.

And in this way, too, the other people continued on for seven more days, walking to Chad, marking their way with graves.

Six of my old friends and I began to scout ahead on our camels. We would take water to the people from the water points we knew. This was becoming critical, because the rain time was over and the little wet spots in the desert quickly dried. We began to find other groups in the desert who needed water, and you must of course help everyone you can. We helped many people to move along, to find one another, to find the safe routes. We brought food from Chad to people who had run out of everything.

We became lost in this work for three months, sleeping in the bush and watching for the white airplanes, the government troops, and the Janjaweed. We buried men, women, and children who could not finish the trip.

Many other groups of men were doing this as well. And in Chad, camps were forming all along the border. Everyone was helping one another, since the world had not come to help yet.

I met two women, around maybe twenty-five and

forty-five in age, who had escaped a village attack, but did so as new widows. They looked behind them to see the men of the village machine-gunned down from helicopters. These two women escaped with two metal boxes, now badly dented. They contained the tools needed by traditional nurses to help deliver babies. They set up a clinic in one of the impromptu camps and were now helping many people every day, long before the first of the white trucks arrived from the aid groups. It was like this everywhere; the best way to bury your pain is to help others and to lose yourself in that.

The sight of the seven of us coming on our camels through the mirages of the desert was strange to people who had been a long time without water and were perhaps a little delirious. They were of course praying for exactly this miracle. It was good to be the miracle, and how can you stop doing that? But we were not always the miracle in time.

"You need to get that baby away from her," some women told me as they swallowed their first sips of water and pointed to a young mother standing alone.

"Her baby is dead and she was carrying it all day yesterday and today. She will not let us have it to bury it," one of them told me.

The little mother sipped water from the cup I held out, and she looked at me very sadly.

"I need to have your little baby now. She has already flown away," I said to her. After a time she let me take the dead child.

Losing a child is so hard, as you may know. It doesn't

matter where you live in the world for that. Babies are usually not named in Darfur until several days or even weeks after they are born, because so many babies die here without doctors or medicine. Those who do not live are considered birds of passage who did not want to stay. Naming the child is therefore saved until it is clear the spirit in this child wants to stay.

We continued to move through this odd landscape of pain, saving as many as we could, and burying others.

We came upon a lone tree not far from the Chad border where a woman and two of her three children were dead. The third child died in our arms. The skin of these little children was like delicate brown paper, so wrinkled. You have seen pictures of children who are dying of hunger and thirst, their little bones showing and their heads so big against their withered bodies. You will think this takes a long time to happen to a child, but it takes only a few days. It breaks your heart to see, just as it breaks a mother's heart to see. This woman hanged herself from her shawl, tied in the tree. We gently took her down and buried her beside her children. This moment stays with me every day.

I felt a need to know something about her from others I would later meet. She was about thirty years old. When her village was attacked by the Janjaweed, she and her two daughters and son—the eldest was six years old—were held for a week. The mother was raped repeatedly. They released the mother and her children in the desert far from any villages. That was probably cheaper than using bullets on them, or else they wanted their seeds to grow inside her. She walked for five days in the desert carrying her children without food or water. When she couldn't carry them any-more, she sat under a tree that she found. There was noth-ing she could do except watch her children die. She took her shawl and tied it to a high branch in order to end her life. We found her that same day, a few hours too late.

After these months, we began to see white trucks over on the Chad side of the wadi; the aid groups that respond to crises were beginning to arrive. We could see them in the distance over the hot desert—sometimes great lines of them. It was time to go talk to them. Things would be dif-ferent with these people arriving. I felt good about this, but my friends didn't know about these groups and had no sense of what they could do. These groups had saved my life in Egypt, so I felt warmly toward them.

My six friends and I had tea over a dinner fire. I told them we should go into Chad and see what these groups could do now. We could help them.

"You go ahead, Daoud, and help your friends in the groups; you speak English and so that is what you were meant to do," the eldest of my friends said. In his kind au-thority I could hear Ahmed. Because of my schooling, my fate would always be a little different from my friends'.

Perhaps because we knew we were about to part, we tossed a little animal bone around in the moonlight, just as we had done as children but a little slower. In the game called Anashel, you have two teams of eight people each. We had three against four that night, but no one cared. Someone throws the bone far away into the sand. Everyone runs for it. If you are the one to find it, you try to run it back to the goal area without being caught and wrestled down, although you can throw it to your teammates. Children play this game at night, when there is at least a half-moon for light and some cool air and no chores left to do. The girls and boys play it together.

There is another game, called Whee, but we were getting too old to play it, so we stayed with Anashel. But so you will know: In Whee you have eight on a team, and try to get your team members across a goal line, as the other team tries to get across theirs. You do battle in the middle, of course. The challenge is that everyone must hold on to one of their feet, so they will be hopping on one leg. This is a very, very hard but very funny game, and it goes on for several hours; you have to be young and strong. The girls would often win because of the work they do carrying water and wood.

On this night, someone finally got the Anashel bone to the goal and that was it for us forever.

I have not described these men carefully because, if I do, they might be killed for what I am about to say, although some are probably dead now anyway. They decided to sell their camels for guns and defend their villages. It was not for me to argue with them.

On that last morning together, we shook hands warmly and embraced one another. While the sun had yet to rise in a very red sky, they rode east toward El Fasher on their camels, and I rode west.

9.
The
Translator

I sold my camel in Tine for what would be about four hundred U.S. dollars and began to move around the refugee camps to help where I could. The fact that I spoke Zaghawa, Arabic, and English made me useful to the aid people who were streaming into Chad. Aid groups are usually called NGOs, which stands for nongovernmental organizations.

I soon had a good network of contacts in these groups and, as a translator, I helped to get refugees to the small amount of help that was at first available.

As far as the Chad government was concerned, the refugees were welcome to come across the border, but they were to remain in the refugee camps, and they were not to work at jobs—even for free as I was doing—since this might take work opportunities away from Chad citizens. This was fair, but it meant I could not be of much help unless I said I was from Chad. So I did this, because it was morally necessary.

As more NGOs came in, and as the camps rapidly expanded, the officials in charge became less willing to look the other way regarding my citizenship. A few reporters began to arrive, mostly from other African nations, and I wanted to take them into Darfur and show them what was happening. I thought I would need some kind of Chad papers to cross the border with the journalists, so I took some of my remaining camel money and went to see my cousins and friends in N'Djamena, who might help me get papers. That is how I became Suleyman Abakar Moussa of Chad. The little scars on my temples were not important; Zaghawa live in Chad as well as Sudan. It was a little strange that I did not speak French, as Chad people do, but many also speak Arabic, so I could manage.

It was a risk, and, yes, I remembered the beatings in the Egyptian jails when I was captured after trying to get into Israel. But you should always do what you need to do to be helpful.

When I was ready to go back to the border area, I went first to one of the big hotels in N'Djamena where the NGOs and reporters often stay when they first come into the area. I had heard that there were journalists there who needed translators to go to the refugee camps and perhaps into Darfur. I was told by a friend who worked in a Chad government ministry to look for a "Dr. John" at the Novotel Hotel. After three days and several trips there and to the other large hotel, I saw some Massalit men I had met in Abéché and who, I knew, spoke some English. The Massalit are a tribe mostly from West Darfur, while my Zaghawa people are mostly in North Darfur, and the Fur are mostly in South Darfur. The two men were in the Novotel's coffee shop, talking to a white man at their table. I went up to them and, in Arabic, asked, *Who is this white man of yours? Who is this hawalya?* That is a not-unkind word for a white person. They explained that this man was looking for translators to go to the camps, and they were going with him. Also, he needed a Zaghawa translator. It seems we had been looking for each other.

"Dr. John, I presume?" is how I introduced myself to him, which I thought was pretty good.

He was not exactly a journalist. He had arrived with people from the United Nations and the U.S. State Department to interview refugees and make a legal determination if a genocide was occurring. If it was not technically a genocide and was instead a more ordinary civil war, that would call for a different international response. For killings to be considered a genocide, the victims have to be targeted because of their ethnic identity.

Dr. John, a young American who looked to be in his late twenties, with blond hair and a bushy beard, said that he was not a doctor, but that this was his nickname. He was glad to meet this Suleyman Abakar Moussa from Chad who spoke Zaghawa, Arabic, and English. After his many questions, he asked if I would be one of their translators for this investigation into possible crimes of genocide. Yes, I would do that. I had found my fate.

10.
Sticks
for Shade

Our caravan of white vehicles, the genocide investigation team, was waved through an army checkpoint at the Brei-djing refugee camp on Chad's eastern border with Sudan. It was one of about ten such camps along the border at the time.

The horizon ahead was fluttering with plastic tarps and little rags tied to sticks for shade. There were shredded green tents and torn white plastic sheeting wrapped around more sticks to serve as tattered roofs and walls. Where the road lifted a bit, this thin line of twirling rags was revealed as a vast city of desperation, as if all the poverty and sadness of the world came from one endless storage yard somewhere, and here it was. This camp had tripled in new souls during the few weeks I had been away. The thinnest shelters flapped everywhere in the wind now. Some were the torn canvas remnants from Rwanda and Sierra Leone and other previous tragedies, rewoven now into a miserable twig and rag nest for thirty thousand birds of passage.

The sight of so many people suffering pushed my own troubles from my head. Because I had been to this camp before, I had been worrying that the people who knew me here would certainly call me Daoud, when the genocide investigators had hired me as Suleyman, citizen of Chad. I was still wanted by the government of Sudan ever since they tried to extradite me from Egypt for immigration violations. If Chad arrested me for false papers or for working illegally instead of staying in a refugee camp, they might send me to Sudan, which would surely be the end of me. This had been hanging over my thoughts as we traveled.

Familiar smells and the low rumble of a great crowd greeted us as we rolled down the windows: babies crying but also children laughing and running after us, stretching out their fingers to touch ours; mothers calling for their children to be careful, the crunch of bundles of firewood being unloaded from the backs of donkeys, the braying of those donkeys, the smoke and smell of a thousand little fires, of spiced and mint teas brewing, of hot cooking oils and overheated, dirty children. A gauze of this sound, smoke, and dust extended over the tangled nest as far as one cared to look, except where the women wore their beautiful colors, which stood out through the sticks: clean and bright reds, oranges, yellows, brilliant blues and greens. The women of Africa, as the world knows, have a genius for color, and they decorated this place with themselves, as they always do. The bold colors they had put away before the attacks were now waving from their lean bodies with defiance—the flags of resilient life.

Perhaps a thousand women and children were standing in daylong lines for their monthly rations of wheat, cooking oil, and salt from the U.N. World Food Programme. Others, with plastic jerry cans, waited in separate lines for their turns at the water pump.

Every day these same girls and women collected wood for their cooking fires by scavenging sticks from the surrounding wild areas. These areas were quickly stripped, angering the local tribes and forcing foraging trips ever deeper into dangerous territory. As a consequence, rape was now the going price of camp firewood. If the women sent their men to gather wood, or if they came along as protection, the men would be killed. So the women and girls went alone and in small groups, often to be raped by the local men. It is the same in Darfur, but there it is the Janjaweed who rape. Many pregnancies of unwanted children were the next tragedy facing these women. The girls and women who looked at us and blinked away our dust as we drove past had the look of people who had seen all this.

Except for the food and the tattered canvas, and for some drawing paper and pencils so the children could make pictures of huts and cows and helicopters shooting people and airplanes dropping bombs and men with bayonets stabbing the people identified in these drawings as the children's uncles, brothers, sisters—except for these, the world's charity seemed almost invisible here. Perhaps the wealthy nations had finally blown themselves away and were no longer available to send their usual token remedies for the problems that their thirst for resources has always brought to such people as these. It should be said that much was being done that we could not see at first glance: groups such as Médecins Sans Frontières (Doctors Without Borders), Oxfam, and Italy's Intersos were hard at work here, but the smoky misery of homeless human beings stretching to the very horizon cannot but upset your heart.

Canvas and plastic make very hot shelters in a desert, and these were what the world had sent—exactly the wrong thing and not nearly enough of it. Perhaps there was no right thing to send; the grass huts of Darfur, so cool in summer and warm in winter, were impossible here because of an insufficiency of grass and wood poles, of space to put them up, and of young men alive to build them. What, indeed, could be built quickly enough for so many? Even so, with all the bright people in the world and so much wealth, could there not be humane shelters for such times if we are a family? Let a peace prize be reserved for those who can someday do this moral favor for humanity.

I had a pretty good idea where my mother and father were hiding at this time, and also my sister Aysha and her children. My surviving brothers were here and there, according to reports from cousins. My second sister, Halima, who had lived near our home village, was with her children in an area that I cannot mention. I was in regular contact with all of them thanks to cousins on the move.

My third sister, Hawa, who lived in her husband's village in South Darfur, had been missing along with her hus-

band and children since the attack on their village. I
thought my new work in the camps might help me find her
and her family if they were still alive. I was looking for and
asking about them always. More than four thousand villages were being attacked and destroyed, so this would be
difficult.

There were perhaps twenty of us in the team: half
translators and half genocide investigators from the
United States, Canada, Australia, and Europe. We translators had been trained for several days to ask questions
without causing further harm to people. I was moved by
the sensitivity of these investigators. Some were very
young, coming straight from universities, while the elders
had worked in Bosnia and Rwanda and other hard places.

The manager of the camp, who worked for one of the
big relief agencies, greeted our team. I stood a little back,
not wanting to be recognized or introduced by my new
name. Our leaders went into the administrator's office and
I felt safe momentarily. But then the woman in charge of
our group got a cell phone call from one of my cousins, who
had tracked me down and wanted to tell me that some of
our other cousins had been attacked the previous day. She
came out and said she had a call for a *Daoud*. Did anyone
know a Daoud?

Some of the other translators knew my secret story and
looked at me. I breathed deeply and smiled, walking forward.

"Some of my friends call me that. Sometimes my
cousins call me that nickname. Daoud is the same name as

David from the Bible. They call me that because I don't mind fighting with bigger men." She still looked a little curious.

"We all have many nicknames," one of my translator friends said quickly to the laughter of others. The woman raised her eyebrows, handed me the phone, and said, "Okay. I get it," and walked back inside. She was going to be cool about these things.

11.
Two and
a Half Million
Stories

We soon split into groups to begin our work. With one of
the investigators, I went to find a sheikh I knew. Each
camp is like many villages pushed together, complete with
their sheikhs. We asked this sheikh to help us find refugees
willing to talk about what had happened to them. As he
took us for a walk, I told him where my sister's village had
been and asked if he knew about her family. He did not.

"There are many other camps," he said in a gentle way.
"Perhaps they are alive and you will find them." I could not
imagine how many times he must have had to say this to
worried people. There are registries of names in each camp,
of course, and I always would check these, but there is too
much confused movement, too much fear and illiteracy,
and too many displaced people—two and a half million
now—for these lists to be complete. The sheikhs, however,
always know better than the NGO lists.

We walked with him through this mass of people. Very

young boys followed us wearing dirty and torn shirts and shorts. They ran around us, bouncing, trying to shake the white people's hands, practicing the few English words they had learned in their now burned schools, or in the roasting canvas classrooms of the camp, or under trees when the school tents had blown away: *Hello, Good morning, Thank you, How are you? What is your name?*

I looked for a boy I met when I visited the camp some weeks earlier. He was about eight years old and wore huge sunglasses that made him look like a small movie star. I didn't see him—not surprising; he was a pebble in this wide desert, as was my sister if she was alive.

Some brave girls joined the boys in their prancing around us, but most walked shyly along the margins of our moving crowd, holding the ends of their bright shawls tightly and sometimes hiding all but their large brown eyes. Older girls and women were coming and going with water and wood, slowing a little to glance at us. A lucky few had donkeys to help them. Donkeys are the best friends of the refugees, and were the only animals many of these families now had—if they had anything. Compared to a camel, which is like a very good truck for the family, a donkey is like a little brown cart, but well loved and well used, and often hugged and kissed every day by the children.

When I was a young boy I loved our family donkey, but in a different way than I loved my fast camel, Kelgi, who was as intelligent as any person I knew. Once when Kelgi was stolen, he walked the thief around in circles through the night so we could easily catch him the next morning.

My father scolded the man and asked his family to pay a debt of some animals, which they did. Father sold these animals to buy us some new clothes and my first shoes. A camel's hooves, by the way, have cracks and other marks as individual as fingerprints, so a camel can be tracked a very long way, and you can see which of your friends has come through this way or that. I cannot say enough about camels. Their milk is a wonderful desert drink—so plentiful and watery that it is often used to pour over your head and arms like a shower after a sandstorm. Camel meat, sadly, is quite delicious and needs no salt.

Like camels, donkeys are loyal unto death. Donkeys suffered terribly as they carried children out of Darfur into Chad. They kept going without enough food or water— three days without water will kill a donkey. A camel, by comparison, will deflate after many days without water. He will get smaller and older looking, with a drooping head. But when he is refreshed with water and grass, he is beautiful again, strong, big, and young-looking again. Donkeys cannot do that. Some donkeys went longer than three days without water, because if there was any water at all, it was given to the children riding on them. When these animals reached the camps and finally felt the children slide down, many of the donkeys straightaway fell dead, having done their loving work. The NGOs in some camps made piles of hundreds of these dead donkeys and burned them in great fires that were terribly sad for the people to see, especially the children. These animals were like family, so full of modesty and devotion.

The donkeys who survived the trip were happy now to be moving wood and water around the camps.

My investigator and I sat on straw mats in the precious shade of a small tree. Seven people, collected by the sheikh as we walked, sat with us to tell their stories. A few wanted the world to know the terrible things they had suffered and demanded that we tell their stories personally to the U.N. secretary-general, whose name they knew. Some thought we must know him as well as they knew their own sheikh. Others were quieter in their pain and spoke to us only out of respect for their sheikh and his request.

Often, then, the stories came pouring out, and often they were set before us slowly and quietly like tea. These slow stories were told with understatement that made my eyes and voice fill as I translated; for when people seem to have no emotion remaining for such stories, your own heart must supply it.

It helps many people just to have someone listen and write their story down; if their suffering is noted somewhere, by someone, anyone, then they can more easily let loose of it because they know where it is. Only little comfort can be given, however, to a woman or girl who has been ravaged. The pain is written deep into her flat eyes and flat voice. There is, she believes, nothing for her now. We would listen with heads bowed, careful to tread only where she would accept another question and perhaps one or two more.

The first day was very hard on everyone who told a story and everyone who listened. The dust of the camp was streaked down the faces of even the most experienced investigators. The coming days would be no easier.

The attack stories were often like my own, though I realized how lucky our village had been to have Ahmed's leadership. So many villages were caught completely by surprise: surrounded, burned alive, massacred from helicopters above and Janjaweed below, with only a few escaping, or a few coming from other villages to find everyone dead and the bodies burned in heartbreaking positions; mothers died trying to protect their children and husbands died trying to protect their wives. Hundreds of thousands were dead. Millions were homeless.

While I was waiting that first evening for the return of some teams who had ventured farther toward the horizon of this great camp, an administrator stepped out of the office and saw me. "Daoud!" he said. "What are you doing here?"

He knew the work I was doing was against the law for a refugee in Chad, so I walked slowly toward him, giving myself time to think. Halfway there, a man in his late thirties, wearing a dirty and ragged robe and head shawl, suddenly appeared from the bush at the edge of the camp and walked toward me. He seemed very intense and maybe a little crazy. Pain came from his face like heat from a little stove. He shook my hand and would not let it loose, patting my hand quietly.

"You are Zaghawa," he said, "and I need to tell you something alone."

He led me a short way into the bush and motioned for

me to sit down with him in the sand, which, under my circumstances, I was very pleased to do. The man's wife approached quickly and pleaded, "He's not right in his head.
Please don't ask him your questions." But I could tell the
man had something he needed to get out, so I asked his
wife if I could just listen to him, like two Zaghawa men
who should be friends anyway. She agreed and stood a few
bushes away, pacing a little and watching us.

They were from North Darfur. Their village had been
attacked and destroyed a few months before my own.

"Everybody ran away as fast as they could. My wife over
there held our two-year-old son tightly in her arms, and
she ran one way through the bushes. Thank God she found
a good way to go. I took my four-year-old daughter, Amma,
and we ran as fast as we could another way around the
bushes. They caught me, the Janjaweed, and I let go of her
hand and told her to run. But she didn't keep running; she
watched from some bushes as they beat me and tied me to
a tree with my arms back around it like this"—he made his
arms into a hoop behind his back.

"One of the Janjaweed men started to kill me in a
painful way. My daughter could not bear to see this, so she
ran toward me and called out, *Abba, Abba.*" These words,
which mean "Daddy, Daddy," filled his throat with emotion, and he paused a long time.

"The Janjaweed man who had tied me to the tree saw
my daughter running to me. He lowered his rifle and he let
her run into his bayonet. He gave it a big push. The blade
went all the way through her stomach. She still cried out to
me, 'Abba! Abba!'

"Then he lifted up his gun, with my daughter on it, with blood from her body pouring down all over him. He danced around with her in the air and shouted to his friends, 'Look, see how fierce I am,' and they chanted back to him, 'Yes, yes, you are fierce, fierce, fierce!' as they were killing other people. My daughter looked at me for help and stretched her arms in great pain toward me. She tried to say *Abba* but nothing came out.

"It took a long time for her to die, her blood coming down so fresh and red on this—what was he? a man? a devil? He was painted red with my little girl's blood and he was dancing. What was he?"

This man had seen evil and didn't know what to do with the sight of it. He was looking for an answer to what it was, and why his little daughter deserved this. Then, after taking some time to cry without talking, he told me he no longer knew who he was.

"Am I a woman who should stay in this camp, or a man who should go fight, and leave my wife and son without protection?" He looked at me as if I should know the answer to his life now. He waited for an answer that I could not give.

"You are still alive," I said. "They didn't kill you."

"What is a better torture than this?" he snapped. "What was better torture than to have to tell my wife and son this?"

His wife came over again and sat near her husband. She picked some small leaves from the shawl that wrapped his head. She told me that his mind was not the same after the attack. "Thank God we have our son, and he is good," she said. "I told my husband that Amma is gone and we must think about the future. But he cannot let go of what he saw."

The woman told me she found a man in the camp who writes and has ink and a quill for that. She had him write down helpful passages from the Koran on small wooden tablets, which were then washed so the inky water could be given to her husband to drink. It is an old cure that often works very well—but had only worked a little for him. They would try again, she told me. Her husband nodded.

When I came back to the same camp a long time later, and I asked the sheikh to help me find this family, the man had gone away, and his wife did not remember me. She seemed more dazed than before. She still had her son, she said, who was at the camp's school that hour. I had come back because the story that would not leave the man's mind was now in my mind, and was in my dreams among other stories, waking me almost every night. I thought that talking to him again might help us both, but now he was gone, perhaps to fight and be done with his life, as I was doing in my own way.

It is interesting how many ways there are for people to be hurt and killed, and for villages to be terrorized and burned, and for children to die in deserts, and for young mothers to suffer. I would say that these ways to die and suffer are unspeakable, and yet they were spoken: we interviewed 1,134 human beings over the next weeks; their stories swirled through my near-sleepless nights. I found that if I made little drawings of the scenes described to me, it would sometimes get the stories out of my head long enough for me to get some sleep. I would wake and make these drawings, and then I could sleep a little. These stories from the camps, mixed with things I had seen with my own eyes, such as the young mother hanging in a tree and her children with skin like brown paper and mothers carrying their dead babies and not letting them go . . . I was thankful that I could not draw them very well—stick figures, really. Even so, it helped.

12.
Connections

When the genocide investigation came to its end, I returned to N'Djamena, Chad, and had a last meal with Dr. John and the others. Genocide is not always easy to prove, so the many interviews were necessary. The United States and others used this investigation to determine that, yes, the government of Sudan was conducting a genocide. The U.S. government did not do too much else, but the American people, as they always do, helped a lot, as did the people of Europe and many other places. The proof of a democracy is surely whether or not a government represents the hearts of its people.

Using the stipend I received from the genocide investigators, I got a cell phone. I wanted a cell number to leave in the camps and with my cousins in case there was news of my family and especially of my missing sister. I also wanted it so I could continue to take investigators or perhaps journalists into the camps and into Darfur. I gave this number to people in the American Embassy and other places: *This is my cell phone number. I speak English, Arabic, and Zaghawa and will take reporters and investigators to the Darfur refugee camps and into Darfur. I translated for the genocide investigators, if you want to talk to them about me.*

Soon after that, I got a call from a group of journalists from South Africa and other African countries—four black men and one white. They were fearless for their stories and wanted to go everywhere to see the violence as it was happening.

I began asking my cousins, friends, reporters, and other well-connected foreigners for the phone numbers of people who could tell us how to travel safely in dangerous territory. My cell phone began to fill with the numbers of sheikhs, drivers, Chad military men, and even rebel commanders—anyone who would help a reporter get in and out alive.

The reporters were so different from the NGO workers. They didn't care about paperwork or the legalities of borders. They just wanted to write stories that would help people. Also, they drank a lot.

If the genocide investigators were like angels from heaven, these reporters were like cowboys and cowgirls coming to clean up the land. When I said goodbye to these African journalists after our trip through the camps and a little into Darfur to see a destroyed village and talk to people fleeing and to some rebel groups, I asked them to tell other reporters to please come write more Darfur stories. They agreed to contact their journalist friends around the world and send them my phone number.

One of my friends told me that some people were asking whether I was really from Chad or was in fact from Sudan. There is always someone to report on everything you do in such places. The fact that we had crossed the border and talked to rebels was soon known by many. Chad and Sudan have a love-hate thing, and at this time they were trying to cooperate. Sudan was telling Chad that I might have been taking reporters across their border. My friend suggested I find some work where I could be invisible. I asked her to call me if it looked like something bad was going to happen. When you start to worry about these things, you see people following you, even if they are not. But maybe some were.

Soon after the African journalists left, I flew from N'Djamena to Abéché in a U.N. plane with two women from New York. Megan and Lori were not reporters, but they were adventurous. To make a difference in the world, they had taken jobs with an international agency that helps women and children refugees.

I told them about the problem with women collecting firewood near the camps and they wanted to interview as many women and girls as they could about that and also about the lack of education for the refugee children. We went to ten camps. Megan and Lori returned to the United States and shared their stories with the Congress, the State Department, and the United Nations to advocate for money for more education in the camps and to provide armed security to accompany the women. This eventually happened for a time, thanks to many others who also argued for this. There is never enough help sent to solve the problems of poor people, but this effort did help many women at some camps. And it made me feel that I could do something.

It is not enough to say we did this and that: you must let me take you into some of these tents. Here is a woman in a small shelter of wood sticks and white plastic, living with her four small children. Her husband and two other children were killed when her village was attacked. Her surviving children often go to sleep hungry because the monthly food ration from the U.N. is not enough. Even so, she always sells some of the wheat in the nearest market so she can buy nutritious foods such as milk, meat, and vegetables. She is trying very hard, but you can see that her children have patches of deep orange in their hair, which means malnutrition. She doesn't have enough blankets for the cold nights, just two thin and scratchy blankets that do not keep anyone warm. There is a big hole in the sheeting where the water pours in when it rains, despite her twig stitching to mend it. And of course she must leave her children to gather firewood.

Three young girls in another tent also must gather firewood. The eldest of these is fourteen. The youngest, maybe nine, wears a dusty black shawl that covers her head like a hood to hide her face. She never looks up and it seems she is willing herself into the sand. They have been raped many times, but they need to go back again soon for more fuel. They cry to talk about it.

Stories like this we heard from hundreds of women and

girls. It might be possible for the wealthy nations or the U.N. to send fuel with the food, or to help the refugees build efficient stoves, but this was not being done.

Lori and Megan slept in a tent each night. They were so saddened by all this that I went to a market stall one evening and got some beer for us to enjoy. The weather chilled the bottles. I knew that you must keep your hawalyas going, and I was learning how to do this. You have to find a way to laugh a little bit each day despite everything, or your heart will simply run out of the joy that makes it go.

I was not always able to do this. A French reporter, and a very good one, was so moved to see the bodies of children after an attack that I could not comfort her. She had children of her own, and could not speak or eat or drink. She could only weep for these children. The sights and smells of death I cannot properly put down here, nor would I want to, except to say that some people must go to hospitals for several days after they experience it.

Later, Megan and Lori sent me books, including an English-Arabic dictionary I still have. They did not send these things because I was a bad translator, but because I told them I wanted to learn English much better. They called my cell phone sometimes to ask about my family and about my missing sister and her family. They had always interviewed me in the way I interviewed so many others, and it was good to have people around who cared to listen and who still had the ability to be outraged and sympathetic.

What Megan and Lori feared most was that I would be sent back and shot before they could hear about it and help.

They were good friends now. It was interesting for me to think that I had two friends in New York. Amazing. And Dr. John in Washington. And more here and there around the world with each new group of reporters.

I had made friends with the right people in the Chad government, who could quickly approve travel permits for reporters. I bought beers for these government people in the outdoor bars of N'Djamena and Abéché. I wanted to make it as easy and safe as possible so there would be no excuses for reporters not to come. If sometimes they wanted to give money to government or military people to make things happen easier, I let them do it, but did not take any of it for myself. This gave me a good reputation with government and military people, since they would get it all. Therefore, when a new reporter arrived, everyone in the Chad government would help me immediately. I hoped that these friends were also losing any paperwork that might cause a problem for me.

One evening at an outdoor bar, a friend said there was the possibility I might be arrested as a Sudanese spy in Chad, so that I could be traded for a Chadian spy held by Sudan. I asked if this was going to happen soon, and I was told that the files on this were being routed the long way around and around, but that this could not last forever.

My brother Ahmed had taught me, with the beautiful example of his own life, how to make friends easily, and in this way he was still helping me.

13.
Nicholas Kristof
and Ann Curry
Reporting

In the summer of 2006 I received a call from New York. Nicholas Kristof of *The New York Times* and Ann Curry of NBC News, along with her crew, needed my help. I soon met them in Abéché. There was a lot of fighting right along the border at that time, so this would be busy and difficult for everyone.

We went immediately to the border town of Adre, Chad, in a convoy of Land Cruisers. This is exactly on the Sudan border, due east from Abéché. Ann wanted to report on the fighting close to Adre, since her big equipment could be set up on the safer Chad side. Nick wanted to go deep to the south along the border to villages that were in the line of attack.

As we made our plans, I saw that Ann and Nick were very admirable people. She was very polite but asked more questions than any reporter I had ever met. Nick looked like a man who gets into trouble. So I went with him.

He wanted to travel first along the Wadi Kaya, the big canyon that separates Darfur and Chad, controlled in most places by the Janjaweed. Nick had a cameraman, a woman assistant, and of course we had a driver. Sometimes we had to drive a little ways down into the wadi, seeing Janjaweed camps so close we could wave to them. We didn't wave, of course; we just drove fast. The driver was very good. The wadi was filled with mango and orange trees, and the vegetable patches of the villagers who had lived there until recently. The fruit was falling unpicked.

After eight intense hours, we arrived at the village Nick most wanted to see. The surrounding villages had been or were being attacked. Nick and his two people thanked me for getting them to the village. Because there are no real roads that you might think of as roads, they couldn't believe how we had even found the place and gotten there safely. But I was thinking that any minute they might not be thanking me.

The sheikh of the village said he expected an attack that night. I wondered if these newspeople really understood that a *New York Times* press pass would not help them unless it happened to be bulletproof. Nick was very casual when I told him we should not unpack too much, and not set up our beds too far from the Land Cruiser. He was as casual as if he always slept in villages under attack.

We could hear shooting in the distance. The sheikh warned me that the trees surrounding the village probably hid some Janjaweed watching us—shots had been fired from there earlier.

I should have mentioned that to Nick, but I didn't

want him to smile at me again like I was *such a worrier*. Besides, there was nothing we could do except be ready to move quickly, which was my job, not his.

The three of them rolled out their sleeping bags while the driver and I talked to the sheikh. The Americans had little flashlights on headbands to help them get their sleeping bags just right. The sheikh pointed to the trees of the wadi again and said I should say something about the headlamps; he said the little lights were saying, *Please shoot me in the head.* Maybe I should have said something to Nick about this, but I decided they would be finished soon and lying down, which was true.

In such situations, of which this was not the first, I preferred to stay awake. The driver and I talked quietly and ate sardines from tins. In the middle of the night, automatic rifles and RPG fire came very close and woke up the sleeping campers, who seemed afraid.

I looked at Nick like *You are such a worrier.* I told them to go back to sleep, that the fighting was still two villages away. Even so, the driver and I stayed awake and counted the seconds between the RPG flashes and their noise.

The next morning we were still alive. After tea we drove to the next village, which had been attacked in the night but had defended itself and survived.

One of the attackers had been captured and badly beaten. He was about fourteen. Another attacker had been shot in his back and was barely alive on the sand at the edge of the trees. His blood was flowing out around him and probably nearly all gone. He was also about fourteen.

These were Janjaweed Arab boys. We talked to the boy who had been beaten. I translated.

"Why did you attack this village?"

"We are from a village just over there. We have always been friends with the people of this village."

"So why, then?"

"We were told by the government soldiers that these people were going to attack our village and kill our families if we did not attack them first. They would give us money if we did this." The money was equal to about two hundred dollars, which was a lot of money—if anyone were ever really paid it.

"Our families need this money, and we had to protect them."

So that is how it was with them. We left the beaten boy with the villagers. They would probably not be kind to him. He was fourteen, as I said.

From here we cut deep into Darfur. The fighting here was heavy and we passed thousands of fleeing women and children as we drove toward the fighting.

"You are crazy!" people yelled at us. "The Janjaweed are everywhere over there. You must turn around!" I should have told Nick what they were saying, but I think he understood; their frightened faces and gestures needed no translation. Somehow, I had no fear myself. Whatever it was that makes a rebel or a government soldier or a Janjaweed feel like he is already dead anyway and might as well just do his job—it was like that. But I worried for Nick and the cameraman, for Nick's woman assistant, and for our driver. For them I had to be as clever as I could not to get them killed.

We reached an abandoned NGO health clinic. Beyond it lay a grassy flat over which people now ran toward us. A village just through the trees was under attack and they were running in panic past us, stopping, remarkably, to urge us to escape with them. Next to the clinic, under plastic shade tarps, were wounded people from a prior attack who had been left behind when the clinic was abandoned moments earlier. Some of those fleeing were wounded, or held their wounded children in their arms. They screamed for medical help that was no longer there. The most seriously injured just sat or lay down around the clinic, some crying or moaning from pain or despair, waiting to die from their injuries or be killed by the approaching Janjaweed. Yet they looked at us and felt concern for us and told us to run while we could.

Nick Kristof, of course, got out his notepad and started calmly interviewing these people. Madness is the business and the method of a war reporter. I breathed deeply and knelt to translate. *This man was shot by his longtime friend and neighbor, an Arab man who had been instructed to collect the gun of this man. When he refused, his friend shot him.*

The gunshots and shouting were getting closer every few seconds. "Nick, we should leave now," I said between every few phrases of translation.

"Just a few more questions," he replied, bouncing from one wounded person to another. I could see some Janjaweed assembling among the trees, waiting for their other men to catch up before rushing the field.

"A very good time to leave," I said again.

"One more quick one," Nick said, flipping the page of his small notebook to make space for the next interview.

Okay, I said to myself, *this is my work.* I translated as the birds in the trees around us now flew away.

The last man interviewed was not wounded, but was huddled there with two small children. He said he was waiting there, hoping that his wife and his other child were alive. She had fallen up ahead. Another man had run to help her, but he had fallen, too.

"Let's go up there," Nick said to me.

Okay. This is my job. We crawled in the grass to the woman. She was dead. The man who went to help her was dead. It was hard to look at them so close.

Nick said that maybe we should get going. He was such a worrier.

As we moved low and quickly past the poor waiting husband, I told him to leave now, that there was no help for his wife and child.

After one last glance at these kindly but doomed people we were running for the Land Cruiser, zigzagging and calling to the cameraman and the woman assistant to jump in the open doors, hearing the gunfire now in the open as we sped faster and faster from the meadow. A child sitting in the grass stopped crying and waved good-bye to us.

We pushed through very deep sand, sometimes with the wheels spinning. "Drive perfectly," I said to the driver. There was no room now for one wrong downshift. We got stuck for several seconds but he calmed down and drove us out. He was too nervous to be driving, but he was in the driver's seat.

We cut through a thick jungle where the Janjaweed lived with their families. This would not be where they would fight if they could help it. Yet here we got stuck very deeply. The young Arab children, maybe one or two years too young to fight, started running over to us.

Like Mr. Thoreau said, when a dog runs at you, whistle. I jumped out of the vehicle and yelled for the boys to come faster, faster, and help! I am your uncle. Help us push this vehicle! They came in a mob and helped us. I knew their brothers and fathers could be moments away. Chug, chug, chug, and we were free and moving very fast toward Chad.

We made it back to Adre, all very tense and tired. Ann and Nick shared their stories. I brought out some Johnnie Walker, which is part of what is done after such a day. I looked at them a lot as they talked. Unlike us, these people did not have to be here. *Cheers to these people,* I said to myself as I washed out my heart for the day, thinking of the child who waved to us from the grass.

14.
Once More Home

You have met broadcast news filmmaker Philip Cox, who saved my dear head from being shot by calling a commander on the phone. Philip had been in Darfur before and knew the dangers well.

He knew exactly what he wanted: this kind of vehicle, this kind of driver, these kinds of foods to take and bottles of whiskey—some for us and some for the soldiers he would interview.

Philip wanted to see where I had grown up and where my village had been destroyed and where Ahmed was buried. So we went there despite the dangers.

After he saved me from being shot, we went to a place inside Darfur where I told him I needed to stop. It was one of the ruined villages of my dreams, the village where the man had been tied to the tree, and his little girl had been killed by the Janjaweed with his bayonet. I found what I thought must have been the tree, the place. It was just something I wanted to do, to say a prayer there for her; after so many dreams, I felt I knew her a little and needed to pay my respects. I wanted to make sure there were not small bones there needing burial, but there were not. I would come to visit this place other times whenever I was near it.

Then we went north through Chad and crossed back into the far north of Darfur. It was a long way to my village. We watched the sky all day, hoping not to see a helicopter or a plume of smoke that would mean a village attack or a battle. When we saw dust from some trucks in the distance, we stopped and let them disappear into a mirage. I made some calls to rebel groups and was told to keep our eyes open because there could be trouble in the area.

We went through the once-beautiful town of Furawiya. Some thirteen thousand people had lived here and in the surrounding villages before everything was attacked and destroyed. This was the picture-book town of North Darfur, with huge trees along its river, and mountains on each side of the sandy bottom that held the town. The destruction had been most cruel. Villagers escaping up a hillside were machine-gunned from helicopters. Philip and I saw the hill still littered with at least thirty-five bodies—many of them children.

We slowed down while driving in the sand along the wadi that had once held the larger market town near my home village. Forgive me for not using the names of some of these villages, but it is to avoid causing further trouble for those still hiding in these areas.

In the wadi there were no bird sounds—so unlike the place I remembered. The silence was deeply spooky. We arrived at the site of the old village, and there we saw some passing rebels resting under trees and others who had always lived in the area whom I recognized.

I showed Philip where the sheikh's home had been, now a black spot in the sand with the remains of some mud-walled rooms. Other patches of black sand were visible up and down the wadi. Some of the larger trees were burned, but newer trees were green and might someday again shade village life in this place.

Philip interviewed some of the rebel troops. A few people who had been living in the secret areas of the mountain valleys, and who were in the village that day to learn what was going on from the rebels, gave me some news: my sister Aysha and my father were nearby and had been told of my arrival.

My father, now very old, was still walking great distances and taking care of animals. I had kept in touch with him. My mother had set up a place in some hidden dry stream and was finding ways to plant some millet, as women do. I wasn't sure if my father was well enough to get to her very often as he moved the animals to grass and kept himself invisible to the Janjaweed and the government troops and their airplanes. But he would have left some animals with her for milk and perhaps some chickens for eggs.

I saw him before he saw me. He was wearing a white jallabiya and a small white cap, all dangerously visible but very traditional. He was more stooped over than when last we met, and a little smaller—the big sturdy body that I had known was almost gone. He was talking to some other older men, gesturing with one skinny arm.

He turned to me as I came near. His eyes were milky and I could tell that he could barely see, but he knew my steps or somehow felt that it was me. We embraced gently. He felt thin and fragile but held me in a very strong way. It was hard to let him go.

"My father," I said.

"Daoud, we have been hearing all about you. It is so good to see that you are alive. You had some trouble yesterday with some rebels."

Darfur is like that. News travels fastest where it seems to have no way to travel at all.

"Take some tea with us," my father said, leading me to a tent. We sat down with the other men, who were uncles and cousins I hadn't seen in these years.

The tent flap later pushed open and my sister Aysha entered in flowing bright green with two children holding her hands. She laughed when she saw me and then just smiled and closed her eyes to float in this moment.

"Daoud, the city man, has come to visit!" she said. "You honor us simple villagers." Everyone laughed. Aysha is the funniest of my sisters.

The tent was soon filled with cousins who wanted to greet me. It was a great joy to be surrounded by family, talking and laughing as if our world were whole again—holding tightly my father's hand, knowing my mother was alive and not far away, imagining Ahmed was out watering the camels. Yet this small tent now held the entire remnant of a once great valley of villages. This beloved world was nearly lost, but here was some of it yet. We ate well; Aysha brought smoking trays of richly seasoned goat meat for everyone. Philip sat with us as part of our family now. He had made this happen, so how could he not be my brother?

Why is it that the person from far away is always the wise expert? For no other reason than this, I was consulted regarding the problem of the day: a young girl refused to marry an older man arranged for her, and she had tried to poison herself. I told them that this girl should not be forced to marry the man, and she might try to kill herself again if this was forced. The men nodded in agreement. The old ways were perhaps bending a little, and this Juliet might be free to marry her true love instead.

That night was the first deep sleep for me in these years since the attack. This was 2005, and the attack had been in 2003—a long time not to sleep much.

Even so, I woke up and stood in the moonlight for a time, waking not from nightmares but from the comfort of this place, which had come into my sleep like the smells of spiced tea and mint. The sands by moonlight looked as they had when I was a boy and played Anashel and Whee late into the night with children now blown far away. Sandstorms will come, covering these ashes in a few years, and who will ever know that loving people lived here, and that the mountain in the moonlight, cool and silent there, is called the Village of God and is filled with all our hopes for our people?

I would like to tell you that Philip and I and our driver made our way safely back to Abéché, but it wasn't exactly that way. It was important to get out of Sudan before dark, and because I would tell the driver to turn here or there, at this tree or down that wadi, he was never sure if we were safe in Chad or again in dangerous Sudan. "Sudan? Chad? Sudan?" the driver was always calling out to me while raising his hands in the air to emphasize his point. Philip thought this was very funny. The driver simply didn't want to be killed that night. And it actually *was* funny after a while. When you are with the British for some time, strange things seem funny. The driver kept going faster and faster as the sun went down. This is not a good idea in a darkening place with no roads. I leaned forward to tell him to slow down, but I was a moment too late: we hit a hole, spun around, and crashed badly. Philip was in front, wearing his seat belt, and was not injured. The driver was shaken but okay. I was in back without my belt, as I was leaning up at that moment, so I crashed headfirst into the driver and broke my nose, which was bleeding furiously as we all climbed out of the wreck. We were in a bad way on the Sudan side, and all Philip could do was point at my nose and laugh. This made the driver finally laugh, also. I started to laugh but it hurt too much. We limped into Abéché and Philip paid the driver in cash for his car. We then found our way to one of the bars in Abéché, which are filled with flies and black market traders. A few drinks improved the pain in my nose and neck.

We discussed only the brighter moments of the trip: seeing my family, of course, and a moment in Furawiya when Philip had stepped close to take some video of an unexploded five-hundred-pound bomb in the sand of the wadi. He had somehow tripped and fallen headlong onto the bomb. He lay sprawled over it for a long moment, wondering if his next move would be a bad idea. I looked at him and thought, *Well, the British would laugh,* so I laughed. He whispered for me to please help him get up carefully, which I was happy to do, since the moment was in God's hands, certainly.

"If it had been me to fall on the bomb, you would have laughed," I said to him in the bar in Abéché.

"If it had been *you* to fall on the bomb, it would have been funny," he explained.

He flew away the next day and I waited for the next reporters willing to brave Darfur.

A call came soon from the BBC. The BBC is a big thing all over the world, but if you grow up poor in Africa, especially in a former British Crown colony, the BBC is a very big thing. They wanted my help. The BBC did. The *BBC.* Amazing. I went to N'Djamena to prepare to meet them. There was a little problem first, however, as the love-hate thing between Chad and Sudan had changed again and rebels backed by the government of Sudan suddenly attacked N'Djamena in Chad. I woke up in that city to RPGs exploding in the streets outside my small room. You do not need an alarm clock to wake up in that city even on a normal morning, but this morning that was especially true.

15.
Waking
Up in
N'Djamena

Though it is the capital of Chad, N'Djamena, a city of about three quarters of a million souls, is located exactly on the country's border with Cameroon, as if it were waiting for the right moment to cross the river and escape its own poverty.

The heat wakes you up in N'Djamena. The children playing outside your door also wake you. I had taken a small room in a low, mud-walled building of eight families, so I can testify to this. Men and boys on camels, riding along the dirt streets to market, shouting from camel to camel, wake you up, too—though it is not unpleasant to hear this as you wake, for the French and Arabic of N'Djamena blend together very musically. Little scrappy motorcycles also wake you up and you can smell their smoke. The old diesel engines of yellow Peugeot taxicabs begin their daily prowl down the mud streets, and their rumble and smoke also come into your room. Many of the women of this city begin their march to the river to wash the family clothes; they talk and laugh as they pass your window. And you might get a cell phone call from friends who want to know what you are doing today.

I normally would open my eyes to my electric fan going back and forth, plugged into the tiny gas-powered generator chirping outside my door. Everyone has one of these generators. Chad has a great deal of oil and a great deal of oil money, but somehow the people only get a few hours of electricity a week.

French fighter jets from their base by the airport fly low and fast over the city on a usual morning. This is a courtesy in case you are still lazy and need to wake up.

The land beyond the town is flat desert with sparse patches of acacia, jujube, tall palms, and, in the summer rain time, a little green grass. Everything is otherwise brown except for along the river, where women lay their bright clothes along the banks to dry after washing them in the clearest currents. N'Djamena is a trading crossroads, so camels, sheep, and goats are everywhere. Some families grow cotton near the river. Some go fishing in the Chari and the Logone rivers and in Lake Chad, once the third-largest lake in Africa—though it is quickly drying up. Tilapia, catfish, and salanga are sold in the town market and fried by women in the open-air bars. It is the best of the many smoky smells of N'Djamena.

Most women wear long, bright clothes—a few wear thin, fluttery veils. The men wear their loose turbans or linen caps. Some wear traditional white robes, the jal-labiyas, but most dress Western style, with matching light brown shirts and slacks. Most people, like me, are tall— I am six feet—and are also a little thin because of all the walking, the hard work, and the dieting that is one of the many advantages of poverty.

You can walk along a mud street in N'Djamena, with old apartment houses beside you, and smoky street stalls selling richly spiced kebab lunches for your only meal of the day, when suddenly you are at the door of a four-star luxury hotel. Chad has oil wells, so there are a few grand hotels for the rich, who come to quickly take the money away before it ruins the charm of our mud and straw cities. I expected to meet the BBC at one of these hotels, but I woke up in an unexpected way and had an unexpected day.

At around three-thirty in the morning, trouble began with terribly loud RPG explosions and mortar and machine-gun fire. The rebels, who were no such thing, but rather the agents of the government of Sudan, swept in from the east, the south, and the north. The Chad Army helicopters hovered over the invasion, avoiding firing where it would hit civilians.

At about five-thirty I could not stand it any longer and went outside. If I was going to die, I did not want it to be from a stray round killing me on my mattress. Let me at least be standing on a street and watching all of it.

Chad Army Land Cruisers were speeding this way and that, and the ragged trucks of the rebels were going that way and this. Young rebel soldiers, not even fourteen years of age, would jump out of the trucks where they could and run into homes to beg for street clothes so they could hide among the civilians. They had been taken as soldiers against their will, drugged, and sent into battle. But some were wise enough to do this dodge, and everyone would help them.

RPG rounds were hitting these trucks full of child soldiers; the streets were filling with the bodies of the dead and wounded. I walked to a friend's house not far away. Trucks of men shooting would go by, but they were not shooting at me. If you were unlucky, of course, you could get hit, but otherwise the soldiers were fighting one another and not the people.

My friend knows many in the Chad Army and they began to call him on his cell phone. This guy was wounded at this address, and that guy was wounded somewhere else. Could you come give us a ride to a hospital? So we, like many other groups of friends, drove madly around the city, avoiding bullets and taking people to the hospitals, which filled quickly but still did an amazing job of helping everyone they could. By noon, all the rebels had been killed, taken as prisoners, or had run away. About 250 young boy soldiers were captured and, I pray, later sent to school instead of to their deaths.

Some 400 troops were wounded in the two hospitals. In the evening, President Déby visited the hospital. It was so loud with screaming and so flowing with blood that the sound and smell of it was impossible for all but the bravest doctors and nurses. The rest of us checked on our friends.

Many people were dead, but after two or three days people found their way back to the markets and outdoor bars to talk it through.

Megan called me from New York; Philip from London; others from all over. *Yes, I am okay.*

The BBC crew arrived in time to interview many of the prisoners and to see the city as it recovered.

16.
A
Strange
Forest

After covering the story in N'Djamena, the BBC crew wanted to go to the camps and then cross into Darfur.

They had come with huge cameras and more boxes of equipment than I thought necessary for any one nation. They would fly to Abéché and I would take their gear by road. I worried that bandits, who roamed in small groups, might rob all these very expensive cameras, lenses, recording machines, and microphones. So I was careful to keep secret my travel times and routes. I asked the passengers on a truck leaving N'Djamena to please put the boxes under their seats as if it were their own luggage, which they were happy to do for a few dollars each.

After we interviewed people in the ever-expanding camps and I made my usual inquiries to the military commanders, we crossed the border. You might think that most of the people of Darfur would either be in the Chad camps or dead, but you must remember how large Darfur is, and how many villages are tucked into every part of it. There were still many villages to destroy and people to kill, as there are even still today. We met crowds of people fleeing everywhere.

At the edge of one village, in a thickly forested place, the village defenders had made their last stand by wedging themselves high in the trees with their rifles. They were all shot and killed. It had been three days or more since the men in the trees had died, and on this steamy spring afternoon, their bodies were coming to earth. We walked through a strange world of occasionally falling human limbs and heads. A leg fell near me. A head thumped to the ground farther away. Horrible smells filled the grove like poison gas that even hurts the eyes. And yet this was but the welcome to what we would eventually see: eighty-one men and boys fallen across one another, hacked and stabbed to death in that same attack.

Reporters are so very human, wonderfully so, and they weep sometimes as they walk through hard areas. There is no hiding their crying after a time. They sometimes kneel and put their heads in their hands near the ground. They pray aloud and will often find a handful of soil to lay on the body of a child, or they may find some cloth to cover the dead faces of a young family—faces frozen in terror with their eyes and mouths still open too wide. They will help bury bodies; we buried many on the BBC journey. But these eighty-one boys and men were too much for everyone.

People vomit when they get close to any long-dead body. You have no control of this, it just happens. And again at the next body. You will soon have nothing in your stomach, but still your body will retch at the sight and smell and of course the tragedy of a life so monstrously wasted. But these eighty-one . . .

Some of the BBC people had to return to Chad, where they were in a medical clinic for three days to recover from what they saw, and smelled, and learned about the nature of what simply must be called evil.

17.
The
Sixth
Trip

I was settling into the rhythm of this work: reporters would call, I would check with commanders in the field, we would go. My next reporter had called months earlier from New Mexico in the United States and was now waiting to meet me.

Paul Salopek is a thin man, about forty-three. For my first meeting with him, I walked into the expensive Le Meridien Hotel in N'Djamena. Its grand lobby has deep armchairs, thick carpets, and African art on the walls. The river that separates Chad from Cameroon runs beautifully behind the hotel, and can be seen through large windows.

In the busy lobby, Paul heard me ask for him at the front desk. He came up and introduced himself and we sat in a quiet corner to plan the coming journey. He had only a few days to visit the refugee camps for an assignment for

National Geographic. We decided to fly to Abéché where Paul would meet with NGO people and I would go to the main market to find a vehicle and driver.

The central market of Abéché contains thousands of market stalls, their tin roofs overlapping to make one great cover over the middle of town. On the south end of this great tin maze you will find about thirty yellow taxicabs waiting. There will sometimes be white Land Cruisers offering rides in different directions, or available for charter. I walked among these vehicles to find a good one, with a good, intelligent-looking driver. I negotiated a fair price and, after stopping for supplies, we picked up Paul at the NGO office. We headed to the camps in heavy rain, and were not making good time because of the deep water in the wadis.

Most Land Cruisers have added to them a snorkel tube running up beside the windshield to allow air to get to the engine when the vehicle is deep in the water. When these vehicles cross a stream, sometimes you can only see the snorkels and a little bit of roof or radio antenna above the water. If you are inside, you must roll up the windows tightly. If you do not know how to swim, you will not be at all bored when the water reaches the tops of the windows. The Land Cruisers used in Africa are larger and heavier than you will see in other places, and some are quite old. This one was old but well cared for. Paul was not worried by the high waters. As someone who does not swim, I am good at rolling up the windows snugly and reminding others to do so.

It is not good to be on these roads after dark, mostly because there are no roads, but also because of bandits and lions and other animals that hunt at night. So I told Paul we needed to find a village soon. We stopped at a Zaghawa village where the sheikh was a friend of mine. After a meal of goat meat and bread, we went outside to the enclosure. The rain had stopped, and the sheikh's people had set up our mattresses and blankets on dry plastic. I fell asleep looking at the stars. This is always the best way to sleep.

I dreamed I was with my eldest brother, who was, in reality, twenty years older than me and now dead—drowned in the Nile, perhaps from a crocodile. In my dream I had somehow fallen into a big wadi and was struggling to get across and keep my head above the water. The thick, muddy current wrapped tightly around me like rope, pulling me away from the shore and from my brother, who was yelling my name and reaching out his long brown arms. I fought the water as hard as I could but my brother's hands were farther and farther away. I woke in the middle of the night clutching the plastic ground cover beside my mattress. It took a long time watching the stars before I got back to sleep.

I woke at dawn to the usual crazy chorus of hungry donkeys, roosters, goats, and sheep, all excited for another long day. I told Paul over a breakfast of green tea that I was worried about yesterday's heavy rains on the road, and suggested we go back to Abéché to let the wadis dry out. He reminded me that he only had a few days, and that we had a job to do. I said okay, and we thanked the sheikh and his family and went on our way in the chirping dawn.

Not far ahead, we had to stop as a red torrent of muddy water filled the wadi crossing our only path. This was the normal place to cross, but it seemed too deep and fast even to trust the heavy vehicle and its snorkel. Chad Army men were on the other side; they had tied a plastic rope between trees on each side of the water, about fifty yards across. The tight line was bouncing on the top of the flood. The soldiers on the other side motioned us across; we were being invited to go hand-over-hand along the rope. "Let's do it," Paul said without hesitation. I wanted to see others do it first.

Other people, with and without vehicles, were stopped on both sides. Women and men with bundles of all sizes wrapped in colorful cloth or plastic were trying to decide if it was worth the risk to cross. Some had no choice. We watched some struggle across. It seemed to take great strength, their bodies flapping on the rope like flags as they grabbed the next handhold and the next, and pulled forward as if drawing themselves out of quicksand.

In fact, many people die each year at rain time trying to cross flooded wadis.

What to do with our vehicle and our driver? The driver could go back to Abéché, of course, and we, once on the other side, could take advantage of the shuttle trips into the next town, Tine, that were being provided by the soldiers. Paul liked this idea.

I remembered that I had some friends who spoke a little English in Tine, and suggested to Paul that I call them. They could meet him on the other side, and I would go back to Abéché with the driver. This was my fear of water talking, of course. Paul just looked at me. "Suleyman, we have a job," is all he had to say. I was Suleyman.

He said he would go first to show me. He stripped down to his shorts and was soon in the water. We found young, strong men who would take his satellite phone wrapped in plastic, and also his camera and cell phone. I could see from his arms as he struggled across that he was very strong. Even so, it was hard for him to make it, and he fell to rest on the other side. He waved me over. Okay. Yes. I would have to think about this one more time.

"You can do it, Suleyman! Hold tight! Keep going!" he yelled over the loud rushing of the flood.

Well, this work was my fate. It was all in God's hands. I could not find someone to carry my phone or little camera, so I wrapped them in my clothes around my neck. This only made the water pull me harder away from the rope. It was very cold; I thought it would be warm. Just holding on to the rope was very hard. That I had to let one hand go so I could move along was a hard idea. I slipped my hands along, inches at time, feeling the rope cutting my hands. My body was stretched out in the fury of the red water. I let my brother help me. I thought of my dream but I let his arms reach impossibly across the water to give me more strength. My phone and camera were already soaked. Paul stood and was cheering my every small bit of progress.

"Come on, man, you have it. You have it. That's it. Keep going."

I made it, of course. My hands were bleeding. I had moved beyond the bad luck that had taken my first brother. I could imagine him floating away into the distance now, his long arms waving goodbye.

18.
What
Can Change
in Twenty-four
Hours?

When our clothes dried, we boarded one of the army vehicles heading into Tine and went straight to the sultan's house there. I knew him from many previous trips with reporters.

We stayed with him a short time for tea and to wash up; the sultan then drove us to the market where we could rent a car and a driver to take us to the Oure Cassoni refugee camp near Bahai, about an hour away. Reporters call it Oleg Cassini, but not because of its appearance.

We arrived after high winds had beaten down the thousands of shelters and the people. Paul asked the refugees what they thought about a new peace agreement signed several months earlier by the government of Sudan and one of the rebel groups. Most people thought it would only create more violence. This was the government's intention, of course, and the people understood. If the government of Sudan wants truly to make peace, they have to provide security for the people. As long as they attack the villages or provoke others to do so, people will resist and join new groups. This is obvious to everyone.

We sat cross-legged under a large tree with ten thoughtful refugees. They described how, since the peace agreement, more villages than ever were being burned, more people killed, more women and girls being raped. It was worse now because there was less protection for the villagers in certain areas. Some refugees wisely suggested that Paul talk to rebels who had signed, and to those who had not signed. But this was a problem, since those who had signed would be following the government's orders now, which included not allowing journalists into Sudan and arresting or shooting whomever was bringing them— like myself. But there were some rebels nearby who had not signed, and we were told how to drive over to where they were.

We called over to them and they agreed to be interviewed by Paul. By the time he finished with his interviews, it was too dark to return, so we slept in their camp.

Back in nearby Bahai the next morning, Paul ran into reporter colleagues while I went to find some spicy kebab in the market and visit with people I might know.

A few hours later, in late morning, Paul was excited to see me return. He had talked by satellite phone to journalist colleagues who had just come back from Furawiya. He learned that a few families, sick of life in the camps, were risking their lives to return to the area. This was a good story, a new twist, certainly. He said we had to interview them immediately. He was running out of time, and the same might be said of those families.

People in the market had just been telling me how dangerous the whole area had become in the last few days. Sudan government troops, Chadian rebels, Darfur rebels, Darfur rebels working for the government, Janjaweed— everyone was fighting everybody in the area just over the border, and sometimes on both sides of the border. No single group held the territory. There was no one to call for permission to come through. This is when it is most dangerous to travel.

But it would be a very short trip. Two hours to Furawiya, two hours of interviews, and two hours back. With luck, we could be back in time for dinner.

The reporters Paul talked to had been able to make the trip. Paul is a very careful reporter; he was getting encouraging information from journalists and the NGO people in town. He had carefully met with these people and even with rebel leaders back in N'Djamena to help him understand the present security situation along the border. What can change in twenty-four hours? Everything, of course. But I remembered my chosen fate. My brother Ahmed certainly did not walk away when things got dangerous.

I called the rebels we had met the night before. They said things were bad now. Nevertheless, I went back to the market to find someone to drive us over there.

A Chadian man named Ali, the son of the local omda, had a new Toyota Hilux crew cab pickup truck with air-conditioning. Ali was a little older than me, very quiet, wearing the traditional white cotton shirt to his feet and a turban around his head.

I looked over his vehicle, which was parked next to other vehicles for hire.

"*Salaam malekum*," I greeted him.

"*Malekum salaam*," he answered.

"*Humdallah*," I continued.

"*Humdallah*," he replied. This is the standard exchange.

I said his car seemed excellent and that I had heard he was a good driver. "I am very good," he replied with no smile.

I explained where I wanted to go with my American journalist.

"I have never been across that wadi into Darfur," he said. "And I think I never want to go. Their fighting comes over here enough."

I explained that the American would pay well and the trip would be short, about six hours. Back before dark tonight. I added, "God willing," which is often said anyway.

"No, I'm scared to go," he said. "I have two children and a wife. It is too dangerous."

I said he would be paid the full day rate, and for two full days. Ali's friends—there is always a swirl of people in such places—began to pay attention to our conversation. "That money is very good," they advised him. "Ali, you should do this. Two days' pay just to run over there and back. You can do it, God willing." As this was hardly the first time I had chartered a vehicle and driver in this market, some of them knew me and said I was very good at all this, and would not go if it was not okay. "God willing," I added.

"No," Ali insisted. "It is not safe to go over there."

His friends now went to work on him. Good money for your family. Back by dark. No Antonovs in the sky and not many refugees streaming across today. Finally, reluctantly, he agreed. I could tell that he was not happy. But it was three hundred dollars, American. That is a small fortune— more than half the cost of a good camel.

We had to leave right away to make it back before dark. We bought some soda, water, and bread for the trip, and went to get Paul. I tried talking to Ali to get to know him. He had served in the army as a young man. A father, as I knew. Son of the omda, which I knew. He was too nervous about the trip to teach me much about him I didn't know.

As we left, I told Paul to keep his satellite phone turned on. I didn't know whom I thought we could call, but it was somehow a comfort. When we reached the wadi that separated the two countries, Ali took us expertly down into the deep water and up the other side. *Tawkelt ala Allah*, I said. *It will depend on God.* Tawkelt ala Allah, Ali repeated. We were in Darfur.

19.
Some Boys
Up Ahead
with a
Kalashnikov

We followed the main lines of tire tracks through the desert. Ali and I glanced out the window often to see if the tracks were new or old, and whether they were from government troops or rebels.

An hour went by; we were nearly halfway there. Ali didn't talk very much. He was extremely tense. We were all very tense.

I most feared a gunman walking into the road ahead to stop us. And in a narrow wadi of a mountainous area, this is exactly what happened. A young soldier, no more than fourteen, stood in the road with his Kalashnikov rifle. A second boy stood nearby. There were most certainly other soldiers all around us among the rocks, waiting for us to try to speed away.

I spoke calmly to Ali, telling him to slow down and stop. *"Mashalla,"* he said into the plastic of the steering wheel, strengthening himself for God's decision. Paul leaned forward from the back to see the trouble. I got out slowly.

The boys wore traditional clothes and had ammunition belts across their chests. I walked toward them. "Salaam malekum," I said. They responded properly, but without warmth, as we shook hands. I pulled a pack of cigarettes from my pocket and lit one. The boys didn't move. "Is there a problem?" I asked them. "No, nothing," one replied.

Two somewhat older boys appeared on the left, also with guns.

"Okay, Daoud, we need you to stand over there by them," one of the two boys who had stopped us said. He knew my name.

The other two boys took Ali and Paul out of the vehicle and were now searching it. They took Paul's satellite phone and our soft drinks. A truck drove up with their adult commander.

"You are finally here," he said to me. This was a bad sign. It meant that there was at least one spy in Bahai or in the other rebel group who told the government of Sudan that we were coming. The government had sent these co-operating rebels to come get us. I could think of no other explanation.

They put us back in our vehicle, with a new driver and the boy soldiers as guards.

Paul asked if I was optimistic. I laughed a little and didn't say anything. We drove for an hour and a half south-east to a place that I knew was near the government-controlled areas.

We arrived at a rebel camp, and a truck with another

commander pulled up. I knew him. "How are you, Daoud?" he asked. "You know the government does not want you here with your hawalya?"

I told him that no one was in control of the area so I did not know whom to ask for permission. We would be happy to go back.

"It shouldn't be a problem," he said.

He walked over to speak to the two commanders whose soldiers had captured us. He talked with them for a long while and then came slowly and sadly back to me.

"They have some authority here. They don't want to send you back so soon." He asked me for a cigarette.

"Things have changed a lot, Daoud; it's not the same. Things are all mixed up right now." He walked away and one of the other commanders came up to tell me that Paul and Ali were to stay in our vehicle and I was to go with him. I asked him what was going on.

"Please don't argue with me," he said. "We are going to take you back to Chad."

I said that I would rather travel with my companions, for whom I was responsible.

"If you go back to be with Ali and Paul, that is your choice, your fate."

If it had been another kind of time, perhaps I would have accepted the ride back to Chad. But my job was to get the reporters into Darfur safely, and to get them out, and nothing else seemed to matter. So it was easy to thank him and go join Paul and Ali for whatever awaited us. Soldiers packed in beside us in our own truck and we were driven a long way through the desert.

"This is not good, Paul." I explained that we were heading into the area where the government of Sudan had its army camps.

Paul wasn't happy to hear this. Ali was sullen. He was always sullen, but now more so.

We arrived at an empty, destroyed village the rebels were using as a base, and were made to sit in an open area by a mud wall. A little food and water was given to us. Ali and I had our wrists tied behind us with thin plastic rope that hurt. Paul was taken in another direction. His wrists were not tied, which I took as a good sign for him.

Ali and I sat there all day, getting hot and thirsty in the sun. In the late afternoon, three vehicles came into the village carrying three rebel commanders. I could soon see Paul talking to one of them in English. He had his notebook out and was interviewing him. Amazing. I laughed a little and pointed with my head so Ali would notice. Paul later walked near us with the commanders and said he believed they would let us go soon. I didn't think this was true, at least not for Ali and me. The mud wall looked like a good wall for shooting people.

It got dark and Ali and I tried to sleep, but couldn't. Two more vehicles arrived late, and several men came over to visit us. They beat Ali with their fists, kicking him a long time with their boots. They did not beat me. They took our watches and our sunglasses, and our mattresses from the vehicle. They took Ali's good shoes. They tried to take my shoes but I did not let them. I said I didn't want to see my own people take my shoes. I said they could shoot me if they needed my shoes, but otherwise I would need them while I was still alive. They went away.

Late at night they pulled us roughly to our feet and pushed us into the back of another truck. Paul was somewhere else—we had not seen him all night. I would later learn that he had been taken away in Ali's truck to the village of Towé, where he would be beaten for three days by young soldiers drunk on date wine.

Ali and I were driven the rest of the night to a place in the mountains, stopping in the morning at a rocky place where tracks go off in a few directions. They made us get out there, so far from any town or village. In this kind of situation you can guess that you probably have about a minute to live. I saw Ali saying silent prayers with his eyes closed. That reminded me to say some, too.

They didn't shoot us. They sat us under a tree and we waited. We got a little sleep finally. Nine rebel commanders soon arrived for a meeting a little ways away in the rocks. I knew two of the men from previous trips, from when this rebel group had not joined with the government. It was raining and each drop of it felt good on my face.

After the meeting, they came over and one said, "There's no problem, Daoud, don't worry." Then they drove away. Two other commanders—field intelligence men—then began shouting at us and beating us with their fists and boots and the butts of their guns. I felt some bones breaking in my fingers where the gun hit me. Then some soldiers tied our ankles and threw us like big sacks into the back of the truck. We continued our journey in a new direction.

When we reached another rebel base, the truck stopped and two men took my feet and two men took my arms and they swung me back and forth high out of the truck onto the rocky ground. When you are tied you can't move to fall the right way, and the sharp rocks open your skin. This was the summer rain time, so there was not even a cushion of dust over these rocks. The same was done to Ali, and I felt so bad for having ever convinced him to make this trip—he was bounced on the sharp road from so high. From this and from the beatings, he had several broken fingers and I don't know what else, maybe ribs. I think he passed out a little after bouncing on the road.

Our lips were blistered from so long in the sun without water. Our arms and fingers were very swollen and painful from the ropes, and now our feet, too. We were dragged under a tree and water was dribbled into our mouths and we were finally untied. We were told that we were waiting for the "crazy commander."

20.
Our Bad Situation Gets a Little Worse

After two hours the "crazy commander" pulled up in his Land Cruiser and yelled at the soldiers for untying us. He supervised the very tight tying of ropes on our wrists and behind our backs. Then he had long ropes tied to our ankles. The other ends of the ropes were thrown over high branches of the tree.

"This is very simple; I will show you how it works so you can do it whenever you need to," he said to the soldiers. Then he turned to Ali and me with a quiet cruelty in his voice:

"I want to torture you two now and you will tell me everything you have in your minds: who sent you, what is your mission, who you are meeting, everything."

Torture was the popular new thing because Guantánamo and Abu Ghraib were everywhere in the news at that time, and crazy men like this were now getting permission to be crazy.

I was first. Three soldiers began pulling the rope, and I was turned upside down hanging from the tree. I thought, *Well, this is not so bad.* After a few minutes, however, it gets very bad. Your eyes feel like they are going to pop out. Your head throbs and you can't breathe. They tightened the ropes on our wrists and ankles for extra pain. Then they tied the long ropes to the trunk of the tree and went away to smoke my own cigarettes as we dangled. The pain gets worse and worse until you finally cry out. I wouldn't have thought this would be so. Of course our injuries were making everything worse—especially for Ali. From time to time they would drop us down and ask us to talk some more.

I told them again and again that I was a translator for reporters, and that the reporters were not spies; I was not a spy, and Ali was just our driver. Ali would say he had been a simple soldier in Chad a long time ago, but he was not spy. He said he had a wife and a small son and daughter, and his only job was to drive people from village to village.

They would say they didn't believe us, and raise us upside down in the tree again. After hours of this, you cannot talk or think. That is when they finally stopped. We were dropped in heaps on the ground.

At around 10 P.M., I woke up in the darkness of the desert. Night insects were busy in our bloody cuts, and this tickling had wakened me.

"Ali. Look. We are alive." I kicked him a little. "It's not so bad." In the faint light of the stars I saw his eyes move slightly.

"Yes, thank you, thank you," he said, blowing a spider

away from his bloodied nose. "This is all very good. Thank you so much for this good trip." We drifted back to sleep.

In the middle of the night two young soldiers picked me up and untied me. They walked me a few dozen steps away from Ali, who was asleep.

"Okay, Daoud," one of them said. "You should go out of here now. Ali is a spy with the Chadian military so he has to stay. But our commander says you should go. Your hawalya has already been sent back to Chad. He was taken to near Bahai and he went across to Chad, and he is waiting for you there."

"That's good about Paul. Thanks for telling me that. But what am I going to tell Ali's family if I go back without him?" I said. "I can't do that. You would not do that. If you were his brothers, what would you say to someone who was responsible for your brother but left him in a dangerous situation like this?"

"Well, you are untied and we are going back to sleep, so we have done what our commander said to do."

I was free to go, but I was also free to untie Ali so we could both make our run for freedom through the mountains. As I untied him, he asked what had been going on, as he had half heard the conversation. I explained the situation, and he insisted that I leave, especially since they had invited me to go.

"This way, you can tell my family where I am and maybe they can help get me out of this," he said. "So you should go now."

I said that I could not face his family if I left him behind, and he understood this.

"They would ask you to pay for our truck," he said, which made me laugh a little because I knew it was probably true. We considered going together, but decided that we would be quickly tracked down and, under those circumstances, killed. So we rubbed some life back into our poor wrists and ankles, and waited for what would come next.

Soon after sunrise, the commander of the base came over, expecting to see only Ali. He saw the two of us sitting untied and talking.

"Daoud. Please come walk with me. I want to talk to you," the commander said.

We walked for a half hour or so. He knew my family and he knew that Ahmed and some of my cousins had been killed when our village was attacked. He didn't like having to kill his own people now that there was this new arrangement, but he hoped for peace someday.

"When the other rebel groups stop fighting us, the killing will stop," he said, perhaps mostly to himself.

"You think that is true?" I asked him. "Why do you think the rebel groups spring up all the time?" He looked at me but could not admit what we were both thinking. He was in all this for himself now, thinking perhaps of getting a promotion someday in the Sudanese Army. War does this to people. There would always be rebel groups as long as the government was attacking villages to push people off the land. Like these rebel groups that were now killing their brothers, he had lost his way and had forgotten his people and was thinking only of himself.

"So, you know Ahmed, my brother Ahmed?" I asked him.

"I knew of him. I may have met him once in El Fasher."

"Okay," I said. I didn't want to do more than bring Ahmed's spirit to walk with us. Maybe it would remind this commander to do the right thing.

He asked if I was sure that I wanted to share Ali's situation. I explained to him the same things I had been explaining all night. He looked sad and left me to go sit again with Ali.

Five soldiers, perhaps only sixteen or seventeen years old, soon came and asked us to stand. I saw the commander drive very fast away down the wadi. He glanced at us as he passed, and he looked to be in pain.

The boys tied our wrists tightly behind us and led us down the road to a tree-lined wadi away from their base. The wadi was strewn with human bones and clumps of hair and the horrible stench of death. This smell can actually stay for many months in such a place, but these bones were new and didn't need to try hard to smell bad. I tried not to walk on these bones but it was impossible. I shuddered at each step. *So, this is where I will die,* I said to myself.

21.
Blindfolds,
Please

Ali's prayers, usually silent, were now loud and clear as the young men took positions four or five steps from us. I recognized some of these boys, but I didn't know their first names. I had known them as small children. From the way they stared back, some of them clearly remembered me. I looked to see who was going to shoot first. A small noise to my left, a sudden movement to my right—each time I braced myself. I called to the boy who looked like their leader.

"Please," I said to him, "can you get us something for blindfolds?"

He asked why we would want that.

"I know some of you boys and I don't want to watch you shoot us. You do what you have to do, but don't make us watch you shoot your own people. We don't have to watch that, not for the last thing we see."

I knew the relatives of one of the older boys—not the

leader—and had seen some of his sisters and cousins in the Touloum refugee camp. I looked hard at him.

"You know, I have seen some of your family in Touloum. Many of them are alive and are wondering where you have been for a couple of years. Some of your brothers are dead, from the same army that you now eat with. You should go find your family in Touloum and help them." I could see he was very moved by this and happy to know some of his family were alive.

The boys retreated a little ways and were perhaps talking about how to make us some blindfolds. They came back slowly, talking about other things and standing around with their Kalashnikovs.

"So you should get us the blindfolds," I said again to the main boy. He walked close to me.

"Daoud, we don't know what you are doing here or if you are spies or not, but we have talked and none of us are going to kill you right now."

"Why is this?" I asked.

"Because we already lost a lot of our Zaghawa people. And now we are having to fight them, which we don't like. We have to do that. But we don't have to shoot you. So we are just going to wait for our commander to come back and he will have to shoot you if he wants to do that."

This was very good. I thanked the boys and they smiled a little. These boys had been through a lot and they still were human beings. Ali was thinking they would shoot anyway, and would not open his eyes or stop saying his prayers, which were of course good prayers and always worth praying.

I asked if we could move away from the bones and go under a tree, and we did. I asked for the first names of the boys, and we talked for an hour about their families. I had news for many of them about their families in the camps. They found some food for us, which was our first in a long time. They untied our hands for this.

"Why does everyone think I am a spy just because I am from Chad?" Ali asked them with a great deal of food in his happy mouth.

The main boy said that Chad was not Sudan. Chad was the enemy.

"You think that?" Ali said. "And you are Zaghawa boys from Darfur?" Because he has two children, he was now talking like a father to these boys.

"Did you know that Darfur was a great country long ago, so great that it was both in Sudan and also in Chad? Did you know that the French, who later controlled Chad, and the British, who later controlled Sudan, drew a line, putting half of Darfur in each new nation? Did you know that? What do you care about this line if you are Darfur men? What business is it of yours if the British and the French draw lines on maps? What does it have to do with the fact that we are brothers?" The boys were moved by this.

"And here is something else for you. Do you know that your people in Chad hear stories about the bravery of the big army you are now a part of—you and your new friends, the Janjaweed?" The boys gathered around him a little closer.

"Yes, your brave new friends attacked a girls' school in

Darfur. They raped forty young girls and their teachers. Some of these girls were eight years old. Fifteen of them had to go to the hospital for a long time, bloody with their injuries. When the nurse working in the hospital told about this, she was taken and beaten and raped for two days and nights. They then cut her seriously with knives. Would you do this?"

The boys looked at one another. "Of course not," their leader said for them. "These would be our sisters." The boys nodded. At this time a heavy rain started and the boys gathered closer under the scrawny tree.

"And if they were little Arab girls?" Ali pressed them. "Would they not also be your family?"

"How would this be so?" the boy asked.

"In the way that they are human beings, and that is also your family." Ali had opened his arms for this and the rolling thunder of the storm gave his speech a wonderful music.

"Yes, of course," the boy said, and in all these boys I could see the light of their souls come back on. The rain, now too much for this tree, washed their young faces.

These boys had not eaten well for a long time. They were discouraged by life and had started to drink bad alcohol made from dates. They had not lived long enough with their fathers to be good hunters and provide for themselves; when they went out on little hunting trips during this time, hoping to shoot a big bird or other game for dinner, we saw them come back with nothing.

Ali advised them that the camps in Chad would feed them and take care of them, and that they could even go to school and find their families, and not have to hurt anyone again. For someone who was no spy, Ali was very good at turning these little soldiers around.

I asked a boy who had been quiet why he was fighting.

"Where am I to go?" he replied. "What do I do? My family is dead, I have no money, no animals, nothing. At least I can eat every day."

"You can go to the refugee camps in Chad, like Ali said," I replied. "They will give you food and you can go to school. That would be good for you."

"No, I do not want to be in the camps and leave my land," he said. "When I die, I will die in my home."

Ali was better at this than I.

When the commander's vehicle came speeding back in the mud, he saw us having our little party and began shouting at the boys. They had not done the thing that needed to be done. He scolded them, but the head boy said to him, "We cannot shoot them. We decided that you have a gun. You are like our uncle, and you will have to do this for us, because it is not right for us to do it."

The commander was pained to hear this. There seemed to be everything in his wet face: anger, exasperation, and maybe some relief. He retied our wrists himself and then walked away, leaving his Land Cruiser running until one of the boys turned off the engine.

In the evening, I was untied and taken to the commander in a mud room that was open to the stars because it had been burned.

"Daoud, you know that if I shoot you there would be trouble between my family and your family someday, so I can't do this. I talked to my cousins and they told me it would be very bad, so here is what we are going to do . . ."

I liked this so far.

"You and Ali need to go back to Chad. So these boys will drive you to another rebel camp and they will take you back from there. So, good luck."

He shook my hand. I was taken back to Ali, and I told him the good news.

"And you believe this?" he said. "You believe they can't find some other boys to shoot us at this new place?"

"That's a good point," I said, "but maybe they believe what we said when they were torturing us and that we are not spies. Maybe they just want us to get out of here. Why waste bullets on us if we will just go?"

He looked at me as if I was very stupid. Indeed, the more I talked, the less I believed my own words.

22.
We Came
to Rescue
You Guys

It was hard to sleep with our hands behind our backs as usual. That night it rained heavy on us. When the rain stopped, some foxes came up to us. We were too tied up to wave them away, so it was not good; there were quite a few of them. But some other animals scared them away—probably wild dogs or jackals. Finally we went to sleep.

In the morning, four of the five young soldiers took us to a camp about two hours away. The boys played a cassette of Sudanese songs and sang along as they drove. When we arrived we were asked to sit under a tree.

Two other young men were tied there. They had been badly beaten. One had a broken arm and was tied at his ankles instead of his wrists.

When we told them our names, one said, "Oh, you are the ones! We came to rescue you guys."

I asked what he was talking about.

"You called us three times and begged us to help with

your truck, and to bring food and water. You said the area was very safe."

"I never called you," I said. Gradually, we figured out what had happened.

The rebels had used Paul's satellite phone to call for some mechanics to come help, and they used my name. This was the rebels' way of stealing another vehicle.

We spent the night under the tree. The next day we were told that all four of us would soon be on our way to Chad. Again we were told that Paul was already there.

Ali had a theory: they could not let us live if they were going to keep our trucks. That would make them ordinary thieves. If we were spies and had been shot, or had been shot in a fight, then it would be okay for them to keep the trucks. So they were going to kill us and didn't want to tell us that.

The young mechanics laughed at him. In their minds, they were already eating food in the Bahai market.

Before we were moved, there was another long meeting of commanders. Afterward, a vehicle approached and Paul was taken out. He was not in Chad at all. He looked exhausted and drawn, and as if he had not eaten since our capture. His face was burned and blistered by the sun.

"Thank God you two are still alive," he said. I told him we would soon be safe in Chad. It was not so far away. Paul shook his head; he did not believe anything they said, especially this. Good reporters smell lies just as dogs smell deeply buried bones.

Paul, Ali, and I were put in one Land Cruiser with its roof cut off; the two mechanics were put in the same kind of vehicle behind us. We began our trip; we headed east instead of west.

The commanders had decided to turn us over to the government of Sudan.

"We are as good as shot," Ali said quietly.

We were driven for an hour to a Sudanese Army camp in the ancient Darfur city of Amboro, the city of my own sultan's home, where his great drum had been beaten in times of war, where good schools and a hospital built by the British in colonial days were now, like the rest of the town, in unnecessary ashes. In their place, soldiers and tanks were everywhere.

Our vehicles stopped near three tanks. When the soldiers went out of the vehicle, leaving the three of us inside for an hour, I told Paul, "I don't know what will happen to you and Ali here, but I know that I am going to die here, so, if you don't see me after this, that is what happened. This is the worst idea the rebel commanders could have for us."

Paul was too tired to say anything. The trip had not helped him.

Soon we were waiting in the sun of the parade ground, whispering to each other. A commander came up to us and stopped in front of me.

"Daoud, you are the biggest problem we have, so we are going to interrogate you first."

Paul, who knew me as Suleyman, was confused to hear me called by another name.

"What is going on?" he asked.

I explained why I used two names in the two countries, and I also told him that I had a problem in Israel that made me wanted by the government of Sudan. I explained that Ali used to be in the Chad Army.

Paul said I should have told him these things. I replied that I could not tell many people. Everything is complicated like that in Africa. Nothing is simple. No one is simple. Poverty generously provides every man a colorful past.

"But you may want to separate yourself from us as much as possible," I told him. Even in such a place a prisoner can demand to be treated separately from the others arrested.

Paul said he did not want to do that. He said he understood about my names and the other things.

"We should stick together," he said. He didn't like the situation, but he was firm about that.

I was then taken away to an interrogation room.

23.
We Can't Think
of Anything
to Say

On the way inside, I decided that I had already talked
enough. These were Sudanese Army commanders now,
the kind of men who had destroyed my village and killed
Ahmed, and I was finished with them. When they started
asking me questions, I told them that I was prepared for
them to shoot me, and I knew they would do that anyway,
just as they had killed my brother and many of my cousins,
but I did not want to answer their questions. I told them
that I accepted my bad situation and they might as well
ask their questions of my brother, as I was with him now. *I
am dead; you know that is my situation and I know that is my situation,
so why should I talk to you?*

Then, for Paul's and Ali's sakes, I said I would recon-
sider this under one condition: If they would bring some
African Union troops, the A.U., in as witnesses, I would
answer any questions truthfully. With the mandate of the
United Nations, the African Union troops were in Darfur—

some barely a mile away—to monitor the peace agreement between the Sudan government and one of the rebel groups. If the government and this rebel group want to attack villages together, or the government and the Janjaweed want to attack a village, or just the Janjaweed or just the government, then that is not the A.U.'s business, though they might make a report about it. They have not been given the resources to do much more than give President Bashir the ability to say that peacekeeping troops are already in Darfur, so other nations can please stay away. Also, African troops have seen so much blood and so many killed that their sense of outrage has perhaps been damaged for this kind of situation. U.N. troops from safer parts of the world, where people still feel outrage, might be better.

Just the same, I thought the A.U. troops could help get out the word that Paul, a noted journalist, and Ali, the son of an important man in Chad, had been taken prisoner. This strategy was something I had discussed with Paul as we were waiting in the sun of the parade ground.

"Let me see an A.U. commander and I will answer all your questions with the whole truth."

They looked at one another seriously—two Sudanese Army commanders and two of the rebel commanders who had brought us in—and then burst out laughing.

"Daoud Ibarahaem Hari—or whatever your spy name is—you are now in the hands of the government of Sudan, and you will talk and tell us everything, even if you don't think so now," the older leader said through the remains of his smile. Spread out on his desk were papers describing all my trips into Darfur, and Internet printouts of all the stories that had come from all the reporters and from the genocide investigation.

"You see? We know everything about you already. We just want to hear you say it."

Paul was brought into the room. He asked me what was going on. I said I had decided not to tell them anything without the A.U. present, even though I had nothing to say that they did not already know.

"They will kill me anyway, so why should I talk?" This was what he and I had agreed to do when we were whispering in the sun. He told them that he also would not talk unless the A.U. were present. They took him away and asked me questions again, which again I refused to answer.

Then they brought in Ali.

"Ali," I said, "Paul and I have decided not to talk to these people unless the A.U. are brought in here. You should do what you think best for yourself, and I will translate for you." Ali did not speak Sudanese Arabic.

"No, I think I have nothing to say to them, either," he said. His attitude toward these people was hardening, and the idea that he would never go home to his wife and children had taken hold in his thinking.

"What did he say?" a commander demanded of me.

"I am not translating for you. Sorry," I replied.

We would all three go out bravely for as long as we could bear the pain of it.

I later learned from two young soldiers guarding us that we were going to be taken to a place where we might change our minds about talking.

"Do you think that will work?" I asked the livelier of the guards. He laughed a little as he looked at me—we prisoners were kneeling in the sand.

"I think you are a hard case," he said. "But they have some very cruel commanders."

A helicopter soon landed in the dusty middle of the camp. Five fat Sudanese generals got out and marched across the sand to meet with the local officers.

"These are the cruel commanders? It looks like they eat all their prisoners," I said quietly to our guards. This made them swallow hard as they saluted the big men.

After half an hour, two of these generals came out to where we were still kneeling in the sun. The largest of them, an Arab man with many stars on his uniform, approached me with great anger in his face. I looked up at him. His round head was like a dark moon rising over his much-decorated stomach.

"You are the problem, here. You, not us, are the war criminal. You bring reporters in to lie about us and bring Sudan down. You are the criminal." The anger that poured out of him was so great that you could see his soul knew very well that he was completely wrong. That is always when anger is the greatest and most dangerous.

He looked at my swollen, discolored hands, laughed a little, and told the guards to tighten my ropes. They saluted and went to work on my bindings, but it was clear to my tingling fingers that they did the opposite.

Paul, Ali, and I were taken to the generals' helicopter and boosted inside.

The two young mechanics who had come to rescue our vehicle were also in this helicopter. The one with the broken arm was in pain as they lifted him aboard.

I shifted around on the hot metal floor where I was told to sit.

We were in the air forty minutes when bullets pierced the cabin with loud pops.

24.
The
Rules of
Hospitality

The bullets bounced around inside the helicopter, finding the back of a young officer. Praise God, it only gave him a good thumping and a big bruise—he laughed when he realized his luck. Perhaps other bullets hit the engine, for the helicopter swerved sickeningly in the sky and the pilot worked the engine at full throttle. The generals, somewhat panicked, shouted at the pilot, asking if he could keep it from crashing. The pilot said he could. *Thank God, thank God,* the frightened generals said to each other. A commander pulled me up from the floor and pushed my face into a bubble window so I could see straight down.

"Where are we?" he shouted over the engine. "Tell me where this shooting is coming from."

I of course knew very well where we were—close to Kutum—but I told him I had no idea. I told him that down on the floor I could see nothing and had lost track of where we were. He kept shouting at me, asking if I wanted to be thrown out; Paul was trying to get them to untie me because he could see I was in too much pain on the floor to help them, even if I wanted to do that.

When everything but the engine settled down, Ali, smiling for the first time that I had ever seen, leaned over to me from his better seat and said it would be good if the helicopter crashed, because we might survive. He asked if I knew how to use a gun. "Of course," I said. Every boy growing up in Darfur goes hunting with his brothers and father. "Me, too," he said. He had served in the Chad Army so he certainly knew how to use a gun. While this talk was a little crazy, I thought, *Well, it is good that Ali is thinking positively.* He was finally cheered by some idea—our helicopter crashing. I joined him in this hope. But within half an hour we were safely over El Fasher, our destination. Here was the town of my high school days. Here was the town of the government's most notorious prison in North Darfur.

As we circled to land, one of the commanders asked if we had been fed at all lately. The young mechanics and I laughed, knowing what he was thinking: that their lapse of hospitality might be the reason for their bad luck in the air. I said we had not been given much of anything. He said we would be properly fed on the ground. The rules of hospitality are very strong here, and sometimes they come to mind at strange times.

I had seen these government buildings often from the road. They looked frightening and imposing to me in my youth, and they looked like death to me now as we came down among them. On the ground, with our hands still tied, we were made to stand outside facing an old adobe wall, painted yellow a long time ago by the British.

A commander shouted at us, inches from our faces. Mostly he shouted at Paul. They made him sit in an old chair while they shouted at him.

"We are going to kill you right now," one of them said. "We will show you who you are dealing with now." They opened their cell phones and waved the screen image of their hero, Osama bin Laden, and the burning of the World Trade Center towers in Paul's face.

It is interesting to me that people bother to shout at you, or even to hurt you, when they are planning to kill you. What lesson will that teach you if you are going to be dead? It has always seemed like a waste of energy. If you are going to kill someone, why not let him go with as much peace as you can manage to give him? I have never understood this, unless it speaks to the mental illness or at least the crazy sadness of these men. So kill us, yes, please do. But don't hurt our ears with your screaming or show us pictures on your cell phones. Just do what you have to do and leave us or our bodies in peace.

But these tortured spirits were stirred up. When these first madmen went inside, others came out and beat us, hitting us on our backs and sides, kicking us, hitting us with their gun butts, warning us not to fall down or else we would be killed. Vehicles were coming and going, but if you glanced at them they would kick you or beat you harder, yelling, "You should not look at these things, you spies."

After a time, the beatings did not hurt as much. I was

only wondering when exactly they were going to shoot us or beat us all the way to death. In the next minute, perhaps? The minute after that?

After three or four hours, I was the first to fall. They dragged me into a large cell where I waited for what would come next. Looking through the old iron bars of the door I watched my friends just outside in the sandy yard: Ali fell next, followed by the boy with the broken arm, then the other boy. Paul was suddenly not there in the chair. When all of us except Paul had been dragged into this room, a guard untied us and gave us a little water.

"You were lucky to fall so soon," Ali whispered through his thirst, a little angry at me for taking this advantage.

The next morning we were taken out to the yard and beaten until we collapsed again. I would like to say that Ali fell first, but I have no memory of that. It is more painful to be beaten a second day, when they are beating on bruises. As before, they dragged us into the cell where we were allowed to rest through the night. The third day they beat us again, but then finally gave us a little food. It really needed salt and oil and was not good. *Acida,* sometimes called *foofoo,* should not be served mixed together with lentils, but especially not without oil and salt. This was meant to upset us. It would be like mixing a hamburger in a milkshake.

We all had terrible pain in our stomachs. It might have been from the beatings or from the hunger, but we couldn't eat much. We learned from the guard that our interrogations would begin the next morning.

I was first. As they led me past the other cells, I saw Paul in one. He looked terrible. I was taken to the office of an interrogator. My legs were tied to the legs of a chair and my hands were tied around the back of it. A large man stood by with heavy sticks and a whip.

"You wouldn't talk in Amboro, that's okay. Do you want to talk now?" he asked.

I had been beaten a lot in the last six days. It was wearing me down, and I knew I was in a place where they could cause incredible pain for me.

"Okay, I will talk," I said, "if you will agree to a couple of things."

He asked me what I had in mind.

"First, you have to tell your guards to stop beating us. Second, if you have a cigarette, you have to give it to me."

"Okay, I'll give you a cigarette. But if you don't talk, the guard here will beat you."

"No," I corrected him, "If the guard beats me, I will not talk. It works like that. I will die."

"Oh, you want to die? Do you know how many people in Darfur have died?"

"I know I would not be the first to die, and if you want to do that, he should beat me and I will die, but I will not talk if he beats me and I will not talk when I am dead."

With this he laughed a little and he got the cigarette out of his pocket—a very expensive brand. He told the guard to untie my wrists so I could smoke.

As I smoked the cigarette, I told him how Paul had contacted me, what Paul and I were doing in Darfur, why I was bringing in reporters, everything true that I could think to say. He said I had come into Darfur six times with reporters. I told him something about each trip, what we saw, the bodies, the sadness of the people, the horrible killing that the government had done to the people.

"When I was with the BBC," I told him, "we saw where you—I don't know if it was you, but maybe it was you—lined up eighty-one boys and young men and hacked them to death with machetes. The smell of that—it was three days old—made the journalists so sick that they had to go back to a clinic in Chad for three days. So maybe that's what you like to do. What the journalists like to do is take pictures of what you do so everyone can see what the Sudan Army does to the Sudan people. We saw where a grandmother had been burned with her three grandchildren. So if you are not proud of this, you should stop doing it. Journalists do what they do all over the world and nobody calls them spies."

I may have said this a little more respectfully, but it was close to this. My memory is bad about this day because of what happened next.

"You should worry more about yourself now," he replied. "Here is what I need to know: When you were talking to the rebels near the Chad border—not the ones who stopped you—you must have seen how many men they had and the kinds of weapons they had. I am going to show you pictures of different kinds of vehicles and different kinds of weapons, and you are going to tell me what you saw."

"I told you I was no spy, but look, you are trying to make me a spy."

"Just talk please. Help me with these pictures. It will be very easy."

I told him that the rebels wouldn't let us drive through their camp, and the only vehicles I saw were some old Land Cruisers, and the only weapons I saw were some old M-14s and very old Kalashnikovs. For most of the pictures they showed me of weapons, I said I didn't think I saw that.

The commander didn't believe me. He gestured to the guard, who started beating me with a thick stick, about a yard and a half long. He then beat me with his fists. I said that they could kill me, but I still would not know about weapons. This beating went on for what seemed like a very long time. I was dragged back to the cell, and Ali was taken for his turn.

He looked at my messed-up face as they took him away. He asked me if it was going to be very bad. I gestured to say it was nothing. He rolled his eyes.

They soon came for me again, because they needed a translator. They knew that Ali had been in the Chad Army, but they were trying to learn if he had been in the intelligence arm. Maybe he had come as a spy. Why would the son of an omda take a job as a lowly driver? They had already beaten him severely before I came. I translated their questions and Ali told them that it was just his business to drive people, and that he had only been a simple soldier in the army. They beat him with the sticks, mostly on his arms and legs and his back and the soles of his feet. Finally I said I would not translate if they were going to beat him. I stopped talking and they kicked and pushed me back to the cell.

They brought me back later when Ali was lying very hurt on the floor, beaten everywhere very seriously.

They told me that I would need to translate some more. I told them that I was finished doing that. I said that I would translate if they would not beat him. They said they would beat him if I did not translate.

"You have just about killed him. You can go ahead and kill him now, but I will not translate unless you stop all your beating of him."

With that, they took me away again. Ali was soon dumped back in our cell—the poor man was only half conscious. He groaned through the night.

We awoke the next morning to nothing. We thought the beatings had stopped, but then we saw Paul coming and going from his cell. This day was Paul's turn. But, thankfully, they would treat him better than they treated us. When we talked in the hall, I did not tell him we had been beaten, as I did not want to add our troubles to his own.

They took Ali and me outside and tied us under a tree. We were almost too sore to move. Paul was later brought out, moving very slowly. He looked very weak, and could only look down. His eyes were sunken. He had refused all food for seven days, demanding that the three of us be reunited. He knew very well that our situation would be hopeless without him. Even though we were now together, he was not going to eat until they released us. I thought this plan would kill him.

That evening, I tried talking to the guards standing outside our barred doorway. I asked them how Paul was doing. One of them seemed willing to talk, so I decided to try to make friends with him. He seemed like he was probably a good man. He gave me a smoke after a while and told me that Paul was in very bad shape.

"Your hawalya is maybe going to die," he said. "Unless you can make him decide to start eating." He put the problem on me.

For several hours I thought about this. When the same guard returned after his dinner, I told him that I could probably get Paul to eat, but they must help me. Soon, a commander came and took me from the cell. We talked on the way to Paul's cell. Paul was on a mattress on an actual bed, not on the floor. It was not a filthy room, just windowless and very old like our cell. The names of prisoners from colonial times were scratched on the walls. Paul looked terrible.

Why did the Sudanese not want him to die? That is a good question. It may be true that they wanted to avoid the trouble that would come with the death of a noted American journalist. But I'm not sure if these people thought like that. I think it was because you only had to look at Paul to know he was a good person, and this brought some human feelings to them.

I had decided to tell Paul something that was not true, only because he is very stubborn and because it was the only thing I could think of to save his life. I told him that if he would accept some food, they would let him make a call to his wife in the United States. He sat halfway up and looked at me.

"Is this true?"

It broke my heart to do so, but I looked at him and said

that it was so. The commander behind me said that it was so. Paul agreed to eat some food.

The commander ordered a soldier to go get him some food, but I said that he must not eat our kind of food, that someone must go into town and get him an American-style sandwich that a white man could eat, and a Coke or Pepsi. There was an argument about the cost of this, but I assured the commander that our food would kill this man, and I truly believed that he was not strong enough for anything but his own food. So two large baguette sandwiches, lamb burgers, were obtained. Even so, Paul would not eat. He instead gave the food to me and to Ali and the two mechanics. Paul would break his fast on his own terms, a day later, after they threatened to force-feed him with a tube. I realized later that Paul had seen through the trick but went along with it to get food for me, Ali, and the mechanics. A good man.

25.
Open House at the Torture Center

From that night things got easier for us. It was possible for us to talk to one another without punishment.

I told the guards about life in El Fasher. My experiences there as a high school boy were not unlike their experiences as young soldiers in a strange place. We agreed that the war and the killing was a terrible time. Some of the soldiers were from the Nuba Mountains, where they had endured their own horrors at the hands of the government they now worked for. *It was foolish for the government to kill our people,* they said. "Good point," I agreed. They were scared young men, with horrible stories to tell. I listened. They would bring me cigarettes, and I suggested that it would be so much easier for us to talk like friends if we prisoners were not tied. So they untied us and let us outside so we could enjoy the cool of the evening. I told them as much as I could about my family so they might think in a new way if they were ever sent to destroy a village.

A great joy came to us when we were allowed to shower and wash our clothes. I cannot tell you the smell we presented to one another after so many days, and the itchy discomfort of our clothes. After about six days you cannot smell yourself, but you can smell the others very well. This shower was a great thing. Paul, too, was recovering, and this helped him. Some nights they let us sleep out in the sand, so much cooler than roasting in the cells.

At around 9 P.M. on the tenth evening in El Fasher, a large, muscular colonel in his late forties arrived at the prison and I was taken into his office. He removed his name badge and covered the nameplate on his desk when I was brought in, probably because he did not want his family to have to answer angry questions someday from my family—this is always on people's minds. That he was thinking I would live to tell about him was a good sign that I might not be killed that day, but it did not occur to me then. I still woke up every morning prepared to die that day; some order would come down and overwhelm whatever little friendships I had made to make our lives easier. We would then be taken out and shot, and our friendly guards would swallow the hurt of this and keep going. They had swallowed far more hurt than this. I saw every arriving vehicle as perhaps bringing that order.

This colonel was the head of intelligence for the western regions of Sudan.

I looked at a bowl of wrapped hard candies on his desk. "Have one," he said, and I did.

"Listen, Daoud. You hold the key to what will happen to you and your friends. You will be busy with us for maybe three hours, maybe six. We will see. If you tell us the truth, you and your friends will live. If you lie to us, you will all die. So it is in your hands." This, of course, is what they say to everyone. "Before I ask you any questions, I want to show some hospitality to you. This guard is going to show you around so you feel at home here."

With that, I was taken by the arm and led down several long hallways I had not traveled before.

In one room was a large chair with electric wires fixed to it. In another room, a chair with restraints was surrounded by medical posters on the wall, helpful torture guides to the eyes, the genitals, the nose, the muscles and nerves of hands, feet, arms, legs. Pictures of eyes, ears, and arms were painted on the walls to remind visitors how easily they could be removed from the body. Trays of steel tools were everywhere.

No person was being tortured; it was all reserved for me and perhaps my friends today. The tour was long and slow and complete, and then I was returned to the chair in the colonel's office. He was smoking a cigarette and taking snuff at the same time.

"So, Daoud, what did you see?"

"I saw the way you torture people and kill them."

"Yes, you did. Would you like to just talk like friends, and we'll stay in this room?"

Under my circumstances, I told him that I thought that was a very good idea.

"Would you like to swear on the Koran regarding what you are going to tell me?"

I told him that would not be necessary, that he could be

assured that I would tell the truth, and that I had always told the truth to them. But I told him I would not talk unless he could agree to something.

He seemed surprised. "And what is that?"

I told him I would need a cigarette. He laughed and pushed one across to me, with a book of matches. He called to the guard to get some hot tea for me.

For the next hour and a half I told the colonel the long story again of how I met Paul, of our arrest on the road, everything. I told him of my other trips with other reporters. Everything I could think of that was true. I knew none of this would be of use to his murdering army.

When I stopped talking, he looked at me strangely.

"This is all the story you have?"

"Everything."

"Daoud, I told you what would happen to everyone if you lied. And you are a liar."

I told him that I didn't know what he meant, that I had told him everything I could remember.

He tossed three pictures across the desk. They were photos of me standing with rebel soldiers and rebel commanders.

"We know all about you. We know your mother's name. We know your cousins. So why would we not know that you were with these rebels?"

I explained that these were trips with Philip Cox, and the BBC, and all of that.

"Well, you didn't tell me all of that, did you? That you met with these rebel commanders?"

"We met with everybody. It was for the news stories. The reporters want to talk to everybody on all sides."

"You didn't talk to me. You didn't talk to government of Sudan commanders, did you?"

"They would kill us, so we didn't. But we wanted to do that."

He started asking me where this rebel group was based, and what another rebel group had for weapons. None of this mattered, as things change so quickly. I told him the same useless things I had told the other interrogators. Land Cruisers. Kalashnikovs. M-14s. I didn't know where they had their bases. We called to see if we could go here or there, I told the colonel, but we didn't ask where they had their bases.

"And it seems the government of Israel asked that you not be sent to Sudan when you were in Egypt. So why do you have such friends in Israel, spy?"

I explained my attempt to find a good job and that it had gone badly.

He was not happy with me, but he had an idea that Paul would contradict me. He had me taken to a nearby room and replaced me with Paul. It was now very late at night. I could hear him interrogating Paul for a long time.

I was brought back in.

The colonel was angry but controlled.

"Daoud, your friend does not want to tell us anything until he sees that you are alive and okay. So we are letting him see you. Now he wants to see Ali. Tell your hawalya that Ali is sleeping and is okay." I told that to Paul.

"So tell Paul he has to talk now."

I told Paul he should not talk unless they gave me an-other cigarette.

"Yes. Tell them that." Paul made a smoking gesture and pointed to me to assure the colonel that I was not mis-translating in my favor.

"You are both in a very dangerous situation. You are in my office. Many commanders come here and are so ner-vous they can't eat or drink. And you just demand ciga-rettes like all this is nothing to you. It is very surprising to me." With that, he handed his entire pack of cigarettes to Paul, who gave the pack to me.

"Get some tea for Daoud," he said to his guards, who ran for it. "And sugar," I called after them.

When the tea and sugar arrived I stood up with the tray and said that, if he didn't mind, I was going to go outside and smoke and drink this tea. Paul stayed to answer more questions, which were of no use to the colonel. I had the guard take me back to my cell after I had drunk all the tea, maybe ten or more cups, it was so good. It was clear to me from almost the beginning of this meeting that the colonel had no power to torture or kill us, or he would have done so. This seemed like a last effort to get us to talk before los-ing custody of us. So we could make our demands and watch what he would do. I think he was a little glad to see some human beings he could talk to.

In the morning, Paul and Ali and I were taken from our cells. The mechanics were taken in another direction. I would never see them or hear about them again until they showed up later to testify against us, and accuse us of spy-ing, no doubt under unimaginable pressure to do so. We were driven to a civilian court in town, our wrists tied behind us.

Our case was being transferred from the military to the civilian court. What was extraordinary was that standing in the back of the courtroom were four U.S. soldiers in their uniforms: a Marine, two U.S. Army officers, and a U.S. Air Force officer. I had some idea that some wheels were turning to do something for us. But look at these guys. My God, you have no idea what they looked like to us. They came up to us, and Paul was very moved to see them. This made the officers very emotional and everyone was wiping their eyes.

Depending on your situation in the world, U.S. soldiers may not always be what you want to see, but for the first moment in all this time, I thought that I would probably not die today. I did not think the danger was over. I knew Paul might walk out with these officers, and Ali and I might be led through another door to the gallows. But maybe not. Certainly not today—not with those guys in the back of the room smiling and winking at us. The good America was in the room.

26.
The
Hawalya

The charges against us were read. I agreed that I had been working with journalists and had entered the country illegally six times. Ali admitted to entering once with a journalist.

It was Paul's turn. He walked to the front of the courtroom. An African Union soldier began to translate the charges against him, but Paul stopped the court.

"I have my own translator. Please bring Mr. Daoud Hari back," he said.

The court was still for a moment, but this was done.

The charges against Paul were ridiculous. He had printed a map of Sudan from the Internet—from the popular CIA World Factbook public website. So he was clearly a spy for them. That sort of thing.

After Paul had rejected all these charges, we were returned to a prison, but a different, civil prison. It was much worse than the military prison, but we didn't care about any of that now. People knew we were there: big people. We were told that Congressman Christopher Shays had been in El Fasher the day before to inquire about our case to the governor of El Fasher. The American Embassy in Khartoum was in high gear for us. We were transferred to the civilian court, which was very good news. The miracle behind this news was Paul's wife and a few others in America who together were making things happen. Paul's many reporter friends were calling powerful people. Reporters I had worked with from the United States, Africa, France, Germany, Japan, and other places were adding pressure. And all of that was added to what the U.S. Embassy staffers were doing.

Paul seemed happy after the court appearance, but not happy with me. He was angry for reasons I did not understand. I couldn't figure it out, so I decided to worry about this problem later.

I talked to the guards a lot. They said we were big news. They gave me a local newspaper with the headline "Three Big Spies Caught." I asked the guards if they thought that was true, and they laughed. I negotiated the use of a cell phone so that Paul could call his wife. The cost of this was Paul's wristwatch, which somehow he still possessed. This was a big moment. He found a corner of the cell for this call and it was very emotional for him. I used the phone later to call a cousin; I asked him to contact my mother and any of my brothers and sisters he could find alive. I asked him to tell them not to inform my father that I was in prison, he would walk through dangerous territory to come see me. He needed to stay hidden where he was.

I could not stop thinking about why Paul seemed cold and angry to me. So I asked him why.

"You have called me a spy to these people. You have done it over and over again when you are speaking in languages I don't understand. I don't know why you would do this—it could cost me years in this prison."

I was amazed. I sat down on the floor of the cell to think. I stood up again and paced around, trying to figure this out. "What word is this? What word do I use to say spy?" I asked him.

"*Hawalya,*" he said.

"My goodness, Paul, that just means 'white guy,'" I tried to explain. But he thought otherwise in his mind. He was also perhaps still a little upset about the Israel and Egypt things in my background that I had not told him when we met.

The U.S. officers interrupted my investigation of this misunderstanding. They brought us blankets and sleeping bags, Cokes, and goat burgers. So this happiness overwhelmed our little problems.

Late in the evening, the attorney general of Sudan came to correct the charges against Paul. He also had us untied; someone had ordered our wrists tied like old times.

The attorney general told the guards to untie the hawalya.

Paul jumped up: "Why do you call me a spy? You know very well I am no spy."

The attorney general corrected him with a smile:

"Hawalya? Sir, it means, well, it just means 'white man.' A white fellow. It's a good word, almost affectionate."

Paul looked like a man who sees a beloved brother come home after being a long time lost to him. He came over to me and apologized and we laughed.

"You are my brother," I said to him. "I would never say things to harm you." He shook my shoulders and closed his eyes and said he knew that.

He seemed more recovered in the next hour than in all the time since ending his fast.

It had been a pretty good day, considering that the three of us were looking at fifteen to twenty years in a very bad prison. But what, not counting family, is more important than friendship?

The attorney general told Paul that his case would be separated from ours. It would make things easier. Paul looked at Ali and me.

"Absolutely not. This will not happen, I assure you," Paul told the man. "We will demand to be tried together. I will ask my country to insist on it."

At this time, though we did not know it, letters from big stars such as Bono and from famous leaders such as Jimmy Carter and Jesse Jackson were piling up on this man's desk— copies of letters sent to President Bashir. The Vatican had even written, and the government of France. When I heard about these things several days later, I hoped that Bashir was a stamp collector, because this would be a good time for him. The attorney general looked upset, but he agreed to this de-mand. In this way, I knew Paul was saving our lives if they could be saved. He had made the same demand with the rebels and with the army, and saved us three times altogether.

It was good that Paul and I had faced and settled our argument. Nothing is more important than friendship in dangerous times. What I did not know until later was that the Sudanese were telling the American consul that Paul's case was something they could talk about, but the two Sudanese men captured with him would be Sudan's business only. It would have been natural for Ali and me to disappear at this point—if not for Paul's demands.

Later that night I could not sleep and I imagined Ahmed came to visit me. He would know all the guards and they would be happy to see him, and they would open all the doors for us so we could take a walk through El Fasher as we had done when I was in school.

It felt very good to imagine walking with him in our old city. I think I had been living like a dead man since he was killed. But I looked around the cell and decided I had some more brothers now, and I should think in a happier way about things.

Perhaps prison was a place for me to think about things. It was in the Egyptian prison where I realized I needed to not be so cut off from my family. Now I was seeing the whole idea of family in a bigger way.

During all my years, Ahmed was always a long step ahead of me. It was still this way in my daydream.

When I saw the guards that morning, I thought, *Oh, yes, it is the part of me like Ahmed that helps me make friends so quickly.* Ahmed has saved my life several times just from that. And if I can find some joy after all I have seen, it will be something of him, too, for you have to love life like Ahmed if you are to truly serve your people.

When I went back into Darfur with my first reporters, the African journalists, I was asked why I was taking the risk, and I told them, not trying to be too dramatic, that I was not safe because my people were not safe—and how can you be safe if your people are not safe? And so who are your people? Perhaps everyone is your people. I was wondering about that.

That next day we were to be moved to the vilest of prisons, where we would wait for trial. The U.S. officers said an American had been badly treated at that prison and a Slovenian journalist had been beaten. So they objected to the move. Arrangements were made for us to stay instead in quarters in the Justice Building. The U.S. officers brought us supplies to make the room very comfortable. They also slipped us some small cell phones in case we were secretly moved—these we were to keep hidden. They also brought us some books and a small DVD player with *Seinfeld* shows. I didn't know about that kind of show, but it was very funny, especially the way Kramer comes through doors. Ali would not watch the shows. He was very certain that we would be taken away and hung or shot at any minute, and he looked at each new day as an opportunity for this. He would jump when any news came to us.

National Geographic put three lawyers on the case and called every day, as did the American vice consul in El Fasher. This went on for two weeks, and still the case dragged on. How long had it been since we were taken at the roadblock? A month and a week or so.

Then some big news. Paul snapped closed his phone after a good call.

"Richardson!" he said.

I didn't know who Richardson was.

"Bill Richardson, governor of New Mexico, which is my home state. He is the man the U.S. often sends to negotiate, and he is very good. He knows President Bashir. He is coming just to help us. Richardson is on his way to Khartoum."

On the day when we expected Richardson might drop by to see us, Paul's wife came instead. I will not tell you how wonderful that was for both of them, and for Ali and for me. That is a story for them to tell, but, really, it was beyond all telling. They walked together in the walled compound of the Justice Building.

That night, in the public area outside the building, where we had a very close view, a man was whipped for some infraction of sharia law. Nearby, a woman had earlier been badly whipped. Her crime was making a fermented beverage and selling it in jars so she could survive. They lashed her twenty-five times until she was unconscious.

We remembered where we were, and we remembered what we do.

"You are supposed to go somewhere now," a guard told us on the thirty-fifth morning of our ordeal.

We were taken in a bright red Land Cruiser to a large mansion, the home of the governor of El Fasher, and escorted inside. Another governor, Mr. Bill Richardson, shook our hands and hugged us. I thanked him for what he was doing. Photographers were flashing our pictures.

As it turned out, we were going home.

I hugged Ali, but he looked seriously into my eyes and said we were a long way from Chad and we should not let them use us for such pictures, since they would kill us after the Americans left. I kissed his cheeks anyway.

The military governor of El Fasher suggested to Richardson that maybe Ali and I could be his guests in this house for a week. I said, "Thank you very much but we think maybe we should be on our way." Governor Richardson winked his eye a little as if to say "good answer."

We flew in Richardson's small jet to Khartoum. Ali was very upset to go to Khartoum, because that was where the government of Sudan could have a good last chance to take us away and shoot us. He threw up several times near Governor Richardson, who was fine with it.

27.
My
One Percent
Chance

A flight from Khartoum through Addis Ababa, Ethiopia, brought us finally to N'Djamena. I relaxed on this flight. But Ali was watching the position of the plane. Could not the Sudanese land the plane back in Khartoum, now that the Americans had left? What was to stop them? He would not be comforted. Even as the plane circled over N'Djamena he was tense, expecting a last-minute problem that would send us back. As the plane rolled to a stop, he could not get off fast enough. On the tarmac, he stopped to breathe the steamy air. He turned to me. "Humdallah. We are home," he said, smiling. I had not seen him smile since he thought our helicopter might crash.

We were greeted by Chadian national security officials. "Come with us," they said. After three hours of intense questions, they released Ali and told me I would have to stay in jail until my situation was cleared up. A friend in the government convinced them to let me go to my little room, which was still waiting for me. It was so good to lie down on my own mattress. So amazing.

The mud wall of my room had always reminded me of the caves we explored as children in our mountain, the Village of God. The cracks in my mud wall seemed to be drawings. The caves of home have drawings, thousands of years old. There is an inner cave with a cool pool of water where children might swim on a hot day. The cave was explored many years ago by the Hungarian man who also explored the Cave of the Swimmers, just over the border from Darfur in Egypt. The book and the movie *The English Patient* were based on his life. He was the only outsider to come see our caves, as far as we know. The caves are still there, of course. Pictures of long-horned cattle and all the beasts of Africa, women and men, children. All the life. So many nights I spent in this room, looking at this mud wall, waking and making my stick pictures of scenes I needed to get out of my head. History. History. History. The people. The little girl. The woman. The child waving.

Over the next several months I would be watched closely by the Chad security officers; several times a week I had to turn myself in for questioning, during which the officers grew ever more angry at me. They were threatening to send me to Sudan in a prisoner exchange. Sudan was telling them I was a spy who was helping the rebels prepare for a new attack on N'Djamena. My jaw had swollen to twice its size from a beating. I told some of my friends that I had fallen, for if they knew I was under the eye of national security they would have kept their distance. A closer friend in the government told me that several groups of prisoners were being exchanged over the next few weeks and I would probably be in the third group.

Despite the way they seemed happy to talk to each other about me, Chad and Sudan were getting close to war again. "Rebels" who were actually proxy troops for Sudan were gathering inside Chad; heavy fighting was going on east and southeast of N'Djamena, where everyone believed an attack would come soon. People packed the bridge to Cameroon; families herded animals and carried bundles of all sizes; honking cars and buses with household goods piled on top and held from windows pressed the crowds along the bridge. Overloaded boats filled the river. Most of the small shops in the city closed, and the sound of the city now was of window shutters being nailed closed.

At this time came the news of my father's death. He had heard about my imprisonment and could not eat. By the time I was free, it was too late for him. The rebels who are not rebels would advance on N'Djamena again. My friends in government would inform me that Chad would soon arrest me and send me to Sudan in exchange for a spy. Megan in New York called and said she would help. A human rights lawyer from Washington called me when he got her e-mail. I was on the phone with him when the rebels were near the city again. I considered crossing the little bridge into Cameroon, but Chris the lawyer said they were working with the U.S. Embassy and the U.N. refugee agency to get me out, perhaps to the United States, where I could continue my work in a new way, and someday return as my people returned. I told him the rebels might be in the city in an hour or so, and that could be bad for me. I said

Chad security might arrest me soon. He said if I went across the bridge all would be lost legally. Ali's family threatened to imprison me unless I could pay for the truck, an expensive truck. *National Geographic* was sending a check someday for that. I finished my call with Chris and closed the phone and said to myself, *Well, so very far away—I give these kind people about a one percent chance of helping me in time.* And then I realized that, for me, that was pretty good. And it was enough.

Leaving Africa was not simple, of course. Even after being whisked from N'Djamena, I had to be interviewed by the U.S. Department of Homeland Security people in Ghana and wait for a letter of transit. A misstep landed me in jail—more waiting. The day finally came. I stood atop a tarmac stairway, looked out over Africa, and smelled the air of it enough to last me for a while. I would work now in other ways to help get the story out and help return the people to Darfur and their homes in peace. What can one person do? You make friends, of course, and do what you can.

To learn more about the author
and the conflict in Darfur,
please visit:

www.thetranslator-book.com.

Acknowledgments

This book is in your hands because editors Jonathan Jao and Jennifer Hershey of Random House saw something about my story in a *New York Times* column by Nicholas Kristof. So if you know these people, you should thank them when you see them, as I thank them now. I did not know how to write a book, but my friends said, "Don't worry, Daoud; we will help you," and they did. So thank you, Megan and Dennis, very much. And I thank Gail Ross and Howard Yoon, who are, respectively, a literary agent and a literary editor in Washington, D.C., who warmly gave me very good advice.

This book is in your hands mostly because I was alive to write it. For this I must thank Philip Cox; Paul Salopek; lawyer Christopher Nugent of Washington, D.C.; Megan McKenna; the amazing people of the American embassies in Sudan, Chad, and Ghana; Lori Heninger; Jack Patterson; Nicholas Kristof and my reporter friends in many countries; my friends in Cairo and an old jailer in Aswan; my cousins in Africa and in the United States and Europe; Christopher Shays of Connecticut, and Bill Richardson of New Mexico; my late father and my late brother, Ahmed; and all my friends in Africa, some of whom I pray will forgive me for mentioning them only by nicknames, which was done to protect them. How in one life can I return the blessings of all this friendship?

If I can presume some bond of friendship between us, my reader friend, let me ask you to think of the fact that tonight as I write this, and probably as you read this, people are still being killed in Darfur, and people are still suffering in these camps. The leaders of the world can solve this problem, and the people of Darfur can go home, if the leaders see that people everywhere care deeply enough to talk to them about this. So, if you have the time, perhaps you can do so. For it has no meaning to take risks for news stories unless the people who read them will act.

—DAOUD HARI
January 2008

Appendix 1
A Darfur Primer

The Darfur situation can be very confusing without a little extra information. This is what you would know if you were almost any Sudanese talking politics with your friends in an outdoor bar or at a university.

When the British left Sudan in 1956 they set it up with a small Arab minority government ruling over a mostly non-Arab African population.

The indigenous Africans had in fact already begun a revolt in 1955, the year before independence was final. The war, mostly in the south, lasted until 1972, when a peace agreement allowed limited self-government for the southern region of Sudan. A Southern Regional Assembly was established for that purpose, and it was to have control of much of the expected oil revenue from the fields just then discovered by Chevron Corporation in the south.

In 1983, after ten years of peace, Sudan's president, Gaafar Nimeiri, nullified this agreement, disbanding the

Southern Regional Assembly and imposing federal rule everywhere. New districts throughout Sudan would be ruled by military governors. The oil revenue, still unseen, would be controlled by the federal government in Khartoum.

Rebel groups quickly formed again. To make things worse, Nimeiri decreed that harsh Islamic sharia law would be imposed throughout Sudan, even over non-Muslim citizens in the south. These laws called for the amputation of hands for minor thefts, for the stoning of women, and many other cruelties. This angered the mass of people, who are quite moderate, and it angered the rebels, who now had three issues: a return to secular government, not sharia law; better representation for indigenous Africans, especially in the south; and a fair local share of the expected oil wealth, including oil jobs and more schools, roads, and clinics.

This political anger joined with the anger of hunger, as these were years of an intense African famine. An uprising in the spring of 1985 overthrew Nimeiri and caused the election of a parliamentary government led by moderate Sadiq al-Mahdi. He suspended sharia law, although it continued to be enforced by some local Arab administrators. Because of the lingering of sharia law, and because the other political issues of representation were still not fixed, the rebel groups didn't disband.

Four nervous years followed. The oil fields could not be put into production during these years because occasional rebel attacks sent Chevron away. Sudan, sagging under heavy debt from the Nimeiri years, could not pay its loans and was cut off from further help by the International

Monetary Fund. Sudan wanted to become a big oil player, but was still a poor relation among the Arab governments. So Mahdi called a new peace agreement that was expected to further subdue sharia law and perhaps reestablish self-rule in the south. That would let the oil production go forward.

Just before the conference, Mahdi was overthrown and exiled by a military strongman, General Omar Hassan Ahmad al-Bashir, who is still in power. He resumed the expansion of sharia law, shut down opposition newspapers and political parties, and imprisoned dissidents. This was a big shock to everyone. I was in high school at the time, and all of us wanted to fight it.

Under the sharia law of Bashir, a woman today cannot leave the country without the written permission of her father or husband. Men and women must sit in separate areas of public buses. The army has been purged of unbelievers. The government-attorney staffs and the courts have been cleansed of those who are not sufficiently loyal to the agenda of Bashir and his right-wing religious brotherhood. Elections have been corrupted. Men and women have been mercilessly brutalized for the most insignificant or unproved deeds. People disappear.

Bashir solved the oil field problem his own way, just as he would later solve his Darfur problem. Many Arab nomads throughout the south had been armed with automatic weapons during the two previous governments as an unsuccessful way of protecting the oil fields from rebel attacks. In the early 1990s, Bashir turned these nomads loose on the non-Arab villages, killing over two million people.

Boys who were out tending their animals far from their villages were the few survivors. They came back to find their fathers dead and their mothers and sisters raped and killed or missing into the slave trade. These boys, after incredibly difficult journeys, found their way to Ethiopia and then to other countries, including the United States, where they are still known as the Lost Boys of Sudan. So the Sudanese government is like this. Bashir is like this.

Communities in the United States, in Britain, and elsewhere in Europe accepted many thousands of these boys and helped them find new lives. This must not be forgotten by Muslims or by anyone.

Bashir built friendly relations with Osama bin Laden and other Islamic radicals, who then opened training camps in Sudan. He turned the oil fields over to the Chinese, who brought their own security people and guns into the now depopulated areas. Here was indeed a good model for economic development without sharing or resistance.

The famine must also be understood, for the weather changes seem permanent now. Beginning in the mid-1980s, nomadic Arabs and the more settled indigenous African tribesmen found themselves in greater than normal competition for the same few blades of grass for their animals, and the same few drops of water in the wells. Arabs drifted south into Zaghawa lands; some Zaghawa drifted farther south into Massalit and Fur tribal lands.

This weather change has created a problem between tribes, and Bashir knows that one of his predecessors lost power because of famine. There are huge reserves of fresh water deep under Darfur. If the indigenous people can be removed, Arab farmers can be brought in and great farms can blossom. Sudan and Egypt have signed what is called "The Four Freedoms Agreement," which effectively allows Egyptian Arabs to move into Darfur and other areas of Sudan. New farms might be a good idea if the water could be used wisely and not consumed all at once, but why not let these farms and farmers develop alongside the returned villages of my people? If the traditional people were allowed to pump this water, which they are not, these farms and this food for Sudan would result.

Throughout these recent years, the Arab government has been promoting Arab identity at the expense of Sudanese national identity. Arabs and indigenous Africans have gotten along for thousands of years in Sudan. Even in my own childhood, we feasted in one another's tents and huts. Any disputes that couldn't be settled through negotiations between the elders were settled in ritual battles held far from any village so that women and children and the elderly would not be harmed. In addition, there has always been so much intermarriage that it is hard to see the differences between the Arabs and the indigenous Africans. Almost every person, at least in the north half of Sudan and in most of Darfur, is Muslim, so there are no religious differences, either. But the drumbeat of Arab superiority began separating the hearts of the Arabs from their indigenous African neighbors. This should remind people of what happened in Rwanda.

Negotiations between elders to resolve tribal disputes were now harshly discouraged by the government. The Arabs were instead given weapons and military support to resolve them. While Arabs were being heavily armed by the government, non-Arab villages throughout Sudan were told to give up all their weapons or be destroyed. Darfur has been thick with automatic weapons ever since the 1980s, when Colonel Muammar Gaddafi of Libya used Darfur as a staging area for his attacks on Chad in an attempt to expand to the south. The Darfuris, both Arab and African, are good traders, and they found themselves with many of those guns. An estimated fifty thousand Kalashnikov AK-47s, RPG launchers, and M-14 rifles came into Darfur and stayed. The villagers, afraid of what was coming, would not give them up.

Darfur rebel groups bristling with this firepower started talking about Darfur independence after the latest purge of non-Arabs from government, and on April 25, 2003, thirty-three rebel Land Cruisers attacked a government military base to destroy the airplanes and helicopters that had been destroying their villages. In retaliation, President Bashir let loose the dogs of war: the green light was given to armed Arab Janjaweed militia groups. Supported by government tanks, machine-gun-mounted vehicles, additional helicopter gunships, and bombers of the Sudan Army, these Arab militias began attacking and burning indigenous villages not in a sporadic way, but in a systematic way calculated to destroy every village and kill every person. Men, women, and children were killed. Village leaders were burned alive or tortured to death in front of their friends and children. Children were tossed into fires. Wells were poisoned with the bodies of children. Everything had come into place, politically, environmentally, and culturally for a genocide in Darfur.

You may remember what I told you of this situation in Chapter 2:

> The problem in dealing with rebel groups is that it is often difficult to know who is on which side on any given day. The Arab government in Khartoum—the government of Sudan—makes false promises to make temporary peace with one rebel group and then another to keep the non-Arab people fighting one another. The government makes deals with ambitious commanders who are crazy enough to think the government will promote them after the war, when in fact they will be discarded if not killed then. These breakaway commanders are sometimes told to attack other rebel groups, or even to kill humanitarian workers and the troops sent from other countries to monitor compliance with cease-fire treaties. This is done so the genocide can carry on and the land can be cleared of the indigenous people. History may prove me wrong in some of these perceptions, but this is how it seems to most people who are there.
>
> It is also believed that the government pays some of the traditional Arab people, many tribes of whom are otherwise our friends, to form deadly horseback militias called the Janjaweed to brutally kill the non-Arab Africans and burn our villages. . . .

This is my prediction: When the government has removed or killed all the traditional non-Arabs, then it will get the traditional Arabs to fight one another so they too will disappear from valuable lands. This is already happening in areas where the removal of non-Arab Africans is nearly complete.

I tell you all this again because even though some people think Darfur is a simple genocide, it is important to know that it is not. It is a complicated genocide.

The non-Arab traditional Africans of Darfur are being systematically murdered and displaced by Bashir's government of Sudan as a part of a program to remove political dissent, remove challenges to power, make way for unobstructed resource development, and turn an Arab minority into an Arab majority.

Can you do that in this century? Can you solve all your problems by killing everyone in your way? That is for the world to decide. Deciding if and when the traditional people of Darfur can go home will also decide if genocide works or not, and therefore whether it will happen elsewhere again in the world. It seems to me that this is a good place to stop it forever.

That will require the repatriation of the Darfur people who were expelled. The camps now in Chad can be moved to Darfur as new towns, bringing schools and clinics and opportunities for personal development to a number of areas that have never had them. From these new towns, village life and some new agriculture can blossom. A zone of protection can be created by the United Nations for this, just as they can be created for other people around the world who need protection in living balanced lives on the earth. In exchange for this protection, the full human rights of the men and women of these areas, the same rights so beautifully described by Eleanor Roosevelt and others in the Universal Declaration of Human Rights, must be added to the ancient customs. The Universal Declaration has long been accepted as international law.

This can be done. What is more important for the world right now than preserving ways of living in balance with the earth?

Appendix 2
The Universal Declaration of Human Rights

On December 10, 1948, the General Assembly of the United Nations adopted and proclaimed:

PREAMBLE

Whereas recognition of the inherent dignity and of the equal and inalienable rights of all members of the human family is the foundation of freedom, justice and peace in the world,

Whereas disregard and contempt for human rights have resulted in barbarous acts which have outraged the conscience of mankind, and the advent of a world in which human beings shall enjoy freedom of speech and belief and freedom from fear and want has been proclaimed as the highest aspiration of the common people,

Whereas it is essential, if man is not to be compelled to have recourse, as a last resort, to rebellion against tyranny and oppression, that human rights should be protected by the rule of law,

Whereas it is essential to promote the development of friendly relations between nations,

Whereas the peoples of the United Nations have in the Charter reaffirmed their faith in fundamental human rights, in the dignity and worth of the human person and in the equal rights of men and women and have determined to promote social progress and better standards of life in larger freedom,

Whereas Member States have pledged themselves to achieve, in co-operation with the United Nations, the promotion of universal respect for and observance of human rights and fundamental freedoms,

Whereas a common understanding of these rights and freedoms is of the greatest importance for the full realization of this pledge,

Now, Therefore THE GENERAL ASSEMBLY proclaims THIS UNIVERSAL DECLARATION OF HUMAN RIGHTS as a common standard of achievement for all peoples and all nations, to the end that every individual and every organ of society, keeping this Declaration constantly in mind, shall strive by teaching and education to promote respect for these rights and freedoms and by progressive measures, national and international, to secure their universal and effective recognition and observance, both among the peoples of Member States themselves and among the peoples of territories under their jurisdiction.

ARTICLE 1.

All human beings are born free and equal in dignity and rights. They are endowed with reason and conscience and should act towards one another in a spirit of brotherhood.

ARTICLE 2.

Everyone is entitled to all the rights and freedoms set forth in this Declaration, without distinction of any kind, such as race, color, sex, language, religion, political or other opinion, national or social origin, property, birth or other status. Furthermore, no distinction shall be made on the basis of the political, jurisdictional or international status of the country or territory to which a person belongs, whether it be independent, trust, non-self-governing or under any other limitation of sovereignty.

ARTICLE 3.

Everyone has the right to life, liberty and security of person.

ARTICLE 4.

No one shall be held in slavery or servitude; slavery and the slave trade shall be prohibited in all their forms.

ARTICLE 5.

No one shall be subjected to torture or to cruel, inhuman or degrading treatment or punishment.

ARTICLE 6.

Everyone has the right to recognition everywhere as a person before the law.

ARTICLE 7.

All are equal before the law and are entitled without any discrimination to equal protection of the law. All are entitled to equal protection against any discrimination in violation of this Declaration and against any incitement to such discrimination.

ARTICLE 8.

Everyone has the right to an effective remedy by the competent national tribunals for acts violating the fundamental rights granted him by the constitution or by law.

ARTICLE 9.

No one shall be subjected to arbitrary arrest, detention or exile.

ARTICLE 10.

Everyone is entitled in full equality to a fair and public hearing by an independent and impartial tribunal, in the determination of his rights and obligations and of any criminal charge against him.

ARTICLE 11.

(1) Everyone charged with a penal offence has the right to be presumed innocent until proved guilty according to law in a public trial at which he has had all the guarantees necessary for his defense.

(2) No one shall be held guilty of any penal offence on account of any act or omission which did not constitute a penal offence, under national or international law, at the time when it was committed. Nor shall a heavier penalty be imposed than the one that was applicable at the time the penal offence was committed.

ARTICLE 12.

No one shall be subjected to arbitrary interference with his privacy, family, home or correspondence, nor to attacks upon his honor and reputation. Everyone has the right to the protection of the law against such interference or attacks.

ARTICLE 13.

(1) Everyone has the right to freedom of movement and residence within the borders of each state.

(2) Everyone has the right to leave any country, including his own, and to return to his country.

ARTICLE 14.

(1) Everyone has the right to seek and to enjoy in other countries asylum from persecution.

(2) This right may not be invoked in the case of prosecutions genuinely arising from non-political crimes or from acts contrary to the purposes and principles of the United Nations.

ARTICLE 15.

(1) Everyone has the right to a nationality.

(2) No one shall be arbitrarily deprived of his nationality nor denied the right to change his nationality.

ARTICLE 16.

(1) Men and women of full age, without any limitation due to race, nationality or religion, have the right to marry and

to found a family. They are entitled to equal rights as to marriage, during marriage and at its dissolution.

(2) Marriage shall be entered into only with the free and full consent of the intending spouses.

(3) The family is the natural and fundamental group unit of society and is entitled to protection by society and the State.

ARTICLE 17.

(1) Everyone has the right to own property alone as well as in association with others.

(2) No one shall be arbitrarily deprived of his property.

ARTICLE 18.

Everyone has the right to freedom of thought, conscience and religion; this right includes freedom to change his religion or belief, and freedom, either alone or in community with others and in public or private, to manifest his religion or belief in teaching, practice, worship and observance.

ARTICLE 19.

Everyone has the right to freedom of opinion and expression; this right includes freedom to hold opinions without interference and to seek, receive and impart information and ideas through any media and regardless of frontiers.

ARTICLE 20.

(1) Everyone has the right to freedom of peaceful assembly and association.

(2) No one may be compelled to belong to an association.

ARTICLE 21.

(1) Everyone has the right to take part in the government of his country, directly or through freely chosen representatives.

(2) Everyone has the right of equal access to public service in his country.

(3) The will of the people shall be the basis of the authority of government; this will shall be expressed in periodic and genuine elections which shall be by universal and equal suffrage and shall be held by secret vote or by equivalent free voting procedures.

ARTICLE 22.

Everyone, as a member of society, has the right to social security and is entitled to realization, through national effort and international co-operation and in accordance with the organization and resources of each State, of the economic, social and cultural rights indispensable for his dignity and the free development of his personality.

ARTICLE 23.

(1) Everyone has the right to work, to free choice of employment, to just and favorable conditions of work and to protection against unemployment.

(2) Everyone, without any discrimination, has the right to equal pay for equal work.

(3) Everyone who works has the right to just and favorable remuneration ensuring for himself and his family an existence worthy of human dignity, and supplemented, if necessary, by other means of social protection.

(4) Everyone has the right to form and to join trade unions for the protection of his interests.

ARTICLE 24.

Everyone has the right to rest and leisure, including reasonable limitation of working hours and periodic holidays with pay.

ARTICLE 25.

(1) Everyone has the right to a standard of living adequate for the health and well-being of himself and of his family, including food, clothing, housing and medical care and necessary social services, and the right to security in the event of unemployment, sickness, disability, widowhood, old age or other lack of livelihood in circumstances beyond his control.

(2) Motherhood and childhood are entitled to special care and assistance. All children, whether born in or out of wedlock, shall enjoy the same social protection.

ARTICLE 26.

(1) Everyone has the right to education. Education shall be free, at least in the elementary and fundamental stages. Elementary education shall be compulsory. Technical and professional education shall be made generally available and higher education shall be equally accessible to all on the basis of merit.

(2) Education shall be directed to the full development of the human personality and to the strengthening of respect

for human rights and fundamental freedoms. It shall promote understanding, tolerance and friendship among all nations, racial or religious groups, and shall further the activities of the United Nations for the maintenance of peace.
(3) Parents have a prior right to choose the kind of education that shall be given to their children.

ARTICLE 27.

(1) Everyone has the right freely to participate in the cultural life of the community, to enjoy the arts and to share in scientific advancement and its benefits.
(2) Everyone has the right to the protection of the moral and material interests resulting from any scientific, literary or artistic production of which he is the author.

ARTICLE 28.

Everyone is entitled to a social and international order in which the rights and freedoms set forth in this Declaration can be fully realized.

ARTICLE 29.

(1) Everyone has duties to the community in which alone the free and full development of his personality is possible.
(2) In the exercise of his rights and freedoms, everyone shall be subject only to such limitations as are determined by law solely for the purpose of securing due recognition and respect for the rights and freedoms of others and of meeting the just requirements of morality, public order and the general welfare in a democratic society.

(3) These rights and freedoms may in no case be exercised contrary to the purposes and principles of the United Nations.

ARTICLE 30.

Nothing in this Declaration may be interpreted as implying for any State, group or person any right to engage in any activity or to perform any act aimed at the destruction of any of the rights and freedoms set forth herein.

ABOUT THE AUTHOR

DAOUD HARI was born in the Darfur region of Sudan. After escaping an attack on his village, he entered the refugee camps in Chad and began serving as a translator for major news organizations including *The New York Times,* NBC, and the BBC, as well as for the U.N. and other aid groups. He participated in the Voices from Darfur tour for SaveDarfur.org. He now lives in Baltimore.